G000066113

Memories
of
Belonging

Memories
of
Belonging

➳

Images from the colony
and beyond

MALAVIKA KARLEKAR

NIYOGI
BOOKS

Published by
NIYOGI BOOKS
D-78, Okhla Industrial Area, Phase-I
New Delhi-110 020, INDIA
Tel: 91-11-26816301, 49327000
Fax: 91-11-26810483, 26813830
email: niyogibooks@gmail.com
website: www.niyogibooksindia.com

Text © Malavika Karlekar
Images © As acknowledged

Editor: Shaurya Shaukat Sircar
Design: Brinda Datta

ISBN: 978-93-83098-59-0
Publication: 2015

Printed at: Niyogi Offset Pvt. Ltd., New Delhi, India

For a tech-savvy generation –
Rajat, Nyla, Ayan, Kiran, Tara, Mallika and Tarini,
enchantments of another kind

꩜

and memorialising
Tony (Nikhil Ranjan) Pal who introduced me to the antique lithograph
Lotika Sarkar and Vina Mazumdar – amazing sisters, friends and mentors

Contents

⌒

Points on a Compass

Wanderings of a Pilgrim and Others

Introduction

I

*I*t is not unusual for serendipity to help imaginations and activate creative spaces. Memories of early rambles through albums and loose collections of family photographs and then, in one's adolescence, an introduction to the work of Thomas and William Daniell, resurfaced many decades later. From the 1990s, fascination with the 19th-century visual led me to owners of much-loved family photographs and to trawls through flea markets and second-hand shops abroad: whether it was a hole-in-the-corner shop by the side of the escalator owned by an elderly expatriate in Singapore, weekend flea markets in Jaffa, New York, Washington and Oxford or established bookshops in Cambridge, I've rarely come away without an old lithograph or map. By 2000, a more than aesthetic interest in the visual medium encouraged me to explore the social and historical context of some of these images and others that I started collecting or observing in books, albums and exhibitions resulting in a series of short articles for the Opinion page of the Kolkata-based *The Telegraph*.

In some cases, the visual became the focus of the article. In others, it illustrated a point or an argument. When I've embedded meaning into visual imagery, I've done so against the backdrop of memoirs and travelogues,

'The Sacred Tree at Gyah, in the Province of Bahar'
Aquatint from Oriental Scenery, *drawn and engraved by William Daniell, 1795–1807*

known as well as obscure, more than 'received' histories and accounts. If I found Bishop Heber's well-known *Narrative of a Journey through the Upper Provinces of India* useful in its discussion of places, people and travel, I've also gleaned from Kamala Bose's *Atmajibani*, fascinating in its account of a young bride of the 1880s' life at camp. Unlike Heber's commercially published two volumes, when she died, Kamala's memoirs were printed by her family.

The 1850s was a momentous decade for India. Not only did governance by Britain change hands but also several new innovations and insitutions from the West found their way here — some only a few years after their discovery. The camera, postage stamp, telegraph, Morse code, the university and railway systems were among the more significant. Others, such as the hill station and the bungalow were concepts developed in the colony — to be adapted later in other parts of various imperial edifices. Hybridity that characterised the colonial encounter resonated in the world of the arts, the interface resulting in many interesting offerings and interpretations.

By the middle of the 19th century, visual representation as a source of information became an important component of the colonial enterprise in India. For the British, relating to the alien land meant balancing the quest for similarities with the principle of difference needed to govern. That cartography, epigraphy and dactylography depended on visuals of different kinds gave a certain salience to non-textual evidence in governance. Woodcuts, copper and later, steel plate engravings were popular methods of reproducing lithographic images.

Paintings by Europeans – landscapes as well as portraits – lithographs and sketches of India had an early history beginning with the 18th-century tours of Tilly Kettle and William Hodges. The most reputed were Thomas Daniell and his young nephew William who acted as a diligent assistant in preparing drawings and sketches for his landscape artist and engraver uncle. Their best known work, the six part *Oriental Scenery,* consisted of 144 aquatints based on hundreds of drawings made during the Daniells' visit to India beginning in 1786. If these were accessible more by the cognoscenti, the popular domain too was soon using images as the basis for cartoons and the ironic was a part of the early history of the visual. Its role in publicising the colonial state and its work was substantial. Yet, not much attention was given to this form of creativity – except of course through the pages of the likes of *Punch* and *The Illustrated London News.* By the 1890s, touristy picture postcards started appearing.

It was, however, the camera that brought the visual into the public domain: it became vital to governance and soon enough to individuals, groups, institutions and families intent on memorialising themselves. The photograph appealed to middle-class sensibilities and families keen to maintain a record of their lives; the official use of the camera and its commercialisation grew almost simultaneously – edging out the monopoly of the landscape artist and portrait painter. Apart from its role in surveillance and control, photography was extensively used by the rulers to record, document and analyse physiognomic aspects of the native population and the country's architectural and natural wealth. Photographic establishments developed the genre of the family portrait, while a small band of photographic adventurers recreated notions of the picturesque, through landscapes and photographs of the Himalaya, its peaks, lakes and cottages built to evoke memories of home with names such as Rose Villa, Gleneagles, and so on. Their 'client base', as Christopher Pinney writes, was more often than not, back home. Pinney is known for his exceptional work on the colonial photograph. The studio soon became a democratic space, available to all who could afford it, irrespective of race, colour or class.

Family albums of the British, their homes in India, local staff, family events and on occasion, shots of those who 'went native' provide valuable insights into the imperial experience. The rulers initially promoted photography for themselves as is evident from the number of freelance photographers and studios started by Europeans that flourished in Calcutta, Bombay and Madras. These establishments – some of which lasted only a few years – made a handsome living out of portraying the trappings of the Raj as well as its well-to-do subjects, aware of the growing fashion of recording themselves visually for posterity or otherwise. Studios and the growing band of comprador photographers replicated trends and techniques being used in Britain. Purveyors of a valued skill, they soon brought the visual into the world of the market and of the urban middle-class home. By the 1870s, the Indian urban elite had started using the services of the photo studio – owned mainly by Britons and Europeans though run often with local staff. A decade later, Indian photographic entrepreneurs had entered the field, the most notable being Raja Deen Dayal in Secunderabad and later Bombay. His studios were well-established destinations for the indigenous nobility, compradors and other notable personalities and their families. In Calcutta, a growing Bengali clientele favoured the studios of S.C. Sen, the Bengal Photographers and Calcutta Art Studio. The more Anglicised preferred Bourne & Shepherd and Johnston & Hoffman.

The ability of the photographic establishment to facilitate, if not encourage, a world of make-believe and role-playing within the studio brings up questions of fantasy on the one hand and of verisimilitude on the other. It would be tempting to say that the camera legitimised mimicry. Certainly where clients used the studio and its props to fantasise and create a mirage-like ambience, there was an element of mimicry. Here clients often knew that they were play-acting, their 'disguised' frame perhaps an

Sarada Ranjan Ray, c. 1880s
Cabinet-size portrait by S.C. Sen studio

important visual device in a cruel world of conflicting loyalties during colonial rule. In other instances, such as the cabinet-size image of Sarada Ranjan Ray, the photograph was a true representation. Known as the 'W.G. Grace of India' (after the famous British batsman), he is reputed to have introduced cricket to Bengal.

'Madras skyline with the High Court and Lighthouse'
Postcard, 1905

The growth of domestic photography meant that families who could afford both the camera and visits to the studio, now had options. It became usual for albums to be crowded out with small format images of picnics, college graduations and even weddings taken by Kodak's ever popular Brownie. Often, the frontispiece would be an elaborate studio portrait of the newly married couple to whom the album belonged. Such photographs too now had informal poses, the body language of conjugality more relaxed than those of early portraits. Images, then, reflected changes in the Indian family, and the photo studio played an important role in documenting these through generations.

By the early decades of the 20th century, at a more popular level, the exchange of picture postcards became quite the fashion, and postcard-collecting often became a favourite hobby of girls and women who carefully organised them in albums. Brightly coloured images were important markers in a growing tourist trade, where visitors bought them in large numbers to collect, send to relatives or even frame. A number of postcards used here are chromolithographs – often printed in Bavaria – of the well-known establishments of Raphael Tuck & Sons and Clifton & Co – large producers of these images for mass circulation worldwide. The black and white ones based on photographs were rare and more expensive.

I I

It would not be entirely true to say that pure serendipity occasioned these articles. Nor for me does image mean only the visual: word–images and evocative descriptions too come within this rubric. And while often a chain of thought was initiated by a compelling visual or text, quite often, I was already working on the framework, a context into which these could be 'fitted'. In many respects, as these articles and the chosen images reflect a historical chronology, they can be read as slightly offbeat musings on certain aspects of this country's history over a century and a half. It was this general, if somewhat rough, historical sense that led me to divide the volume into three sections: the first sets the stage for the appearance of the colonial state – not through the usual tropes of political and economic domination but more with vignettes about a few institutions and people's personal choices, interests and indeed obsessions. The second section is a whimsical journey through India – from north to south and east to west. While I did try to choose towns, cities and other spaces keeping in mind the need to 'represent' the country, there are many omissions and some places and areas might appear to get more attention than others. I've skimmed through this vast country somewhat like an impressionist at her easel, making some hard choices on the way. It was also a question of being able to garner the right image and the most evocative account of a place; even while conceding that such volumes are cornucopias of information and some anecdotes, Murray's *Handbooks* and the invaluable district gazetteer-style of writing do have their limitations. While I have read some of these and used information from them, I chose to base my articles on more personal accounts of the

'Noble Amherstia'
Watercolour illustration in Some Beautiful Indian Trees *by*
Ethelbert Blatter and Walter Samuel Millard, 1937

times. The final section is all about modes of travel and, as various types of locomotion 'belonged' to certain time periods in the country's evolution, this too is like a potted history of a century and a half of people on the move, beginning with the *palki* and ending with experiences of the railways.

The colonial state and its emerging institutions as well as avocations of significant men interested me – and these are discussed in the first section. Who knew, for instance, that William Carey hankered for the English daisy or that A.O. Hume's real inclination was not in politics or the bureaucracy but in roaming free in the countryside, observing birds? Viceroy Curzon's interest in monuments has been well documented – though what is not much known is that he prided himself as a bit of a garden designer. Digging for archaeological finds as well experimenting with architectural styles – both domestic as well as institutional – were very popular, and in fact, encouraged by the rulers. The dominant leitmotif of the imperial presence was certainly governance – but in order to keep the bureaucratic and political behemoth going it was essential to ensure that the rulers and their families felt 'at home'. Domestic architecture in the form of the bungalow – a unique blend of western-style bedrooms, attached dressing rooms and bathrooms with the verandas and courtyards of the East all neatly contained within a compound – could hardly be complete without a garden with neatly laid out beds and borders. The compound with its gates and driveway helped maintain the boundary between the teeming life of 'native' India and the enclaves of the rulers.

Women were rarely memorialised as initiators of things away from the domestic space; hence their excellence in homemaking and in the garden were noted – and Gertrude Jekyll's expertise and innovations in garden design found a natural resonance in the colonies. Though Jekyll did not come to India, her influence in bungalow gardens was quite evident. Her emphasis on the need to blend exotics – in the colony, flowers of the traditional English garden – with natives, found expression in the garden and home culture of the rulers in India. It was in the hill stations that the English garden found appropriate expression with rambling roses, summer annuals, the willow and the local river as a substitute for a 'babbling brook'. Flora Annie Steel and Grace Gardiner's *The Complete Indian Housekeeper and Cook*, though dismissive of 'native gardeners', were all for hanging baskets and gardens reminiscent of home. Memoirs and letters of Emily Eden, Sarah Amherst, Charlotte Canning and others have interesting nuggets on the horticultural grandeur of those days set in a hostile and febrile climate. In fact, the *Amherstia Nobilis*, a flowering tree with a profusion of large scarlet flowers, is named after Lady Sarah Amherst. Wife of Governor-General William Amherst, she was an avid early 19th-century plant collector. If hill stations became retreats from the interminable heat and dust of the Indian plains, they also provided access to the higher reaches of the Himalaya in the north and the ghats and the Nilgiris further south. Trekking and exploration became favoured pastimes, and mountaineering a serious pursuit among some who like George Mallory hoped to climb 'from the heart' (Macfarlane). British imperialism clearly had something to do with the desire to conquer the unknown mountain as well. Or to re-model existing memorials, legacies of earlier empires.

Not unexpectedly, gardens played a significant role in the memorials built after 1857 – round the Memorial Well at Cawnpore (Kanpur), Lucknow's Residency as well as other sites in Delhi. However, the memorial that excited the colonial imagination the most – in particular that of George Nathaniel Curzon – was Taj Mahal. If Mallory was obsessed with Everest, Curzon's fixation was with the Taj. The restoration of the mausoleum (thankfully it did not require too much work) was left to the Archaeological Survey of India while the gardens were of far greater interest to the viceroy. Curzon removed the original dense foliage and soon converted what had been a classic Mughal garden into an English park where low cypresses afford an unobstructed view of the monument from afar.

George Nathaniel Curzon had visited India more than once before he became viceroy in 1899. A compulsive traveller, his fascination with discovery led him to the source of Amu Darya River in Uzbekistan – for which a duly impressed Royal Geographical Society awarded him a gold medal. Curzon had many admirers, followers and detractors – and Francis Younghusband was among the former. One of Curzon's most assiduous and keen-eyed officers, Younghusband took time off from his official work that included high-level espionage, to travel in Kashmir and write about his experiences; the British had an early fascination with the North-West Frontier and Lilah Wingfield could not resist the temptation of trying to retrace at least some of Lady Florentina Sale's journey into Afghanistan. Lilah led a charmed life and was nowhere near being imprisoned – but she nevertheless wrote of tonga rides in hopeless terrains.

From a Photo. by F. Frith & Co

THE TAJ MAHAL, AGRA.

'The Taj Mahal, Agra.'
Postcard by Frith & Co based on an etching, c. 1890s

Delhi in the early 1920s was also host to the tonga as well as the home of an established elite of north Indian upper-caste families. The talented cousins, Sheila Dhar and Madhur Jaffrey provide fascinating accounts of childhoods touched at the fringes by rapid political and social change. Prior to 1911 and the shift of the capital from Calcutta to Delhi, it was in the three Presidencies that the imperial presence was felt the most. Calcutta, Darjeeling, Benares (Varanasi) could not but be written about as well as visualised in great detail by colonial travellers and artists such as the Daniells' in their *Views of Calcutta*. A few decades later, indigenous artists on the footpaths of the traditional Kalighat temple were honing their skills in lampooning, producing caricatures as well as representations of the Hindu pantheon for the faithful. In Bombay, the classic Gothic was modified to suit the climate and its growing 'native' elite. A polyglot population, an active theatre movement and educated Muslim women who enjoyed maintaining a family journal all thrived in the metropolis of gracious avenues, a sweeping oceanside promenade and stately family homes. As one travelled southwards towards Madras and Pondicherry, architectural styles changed, the interesting synthesising at times with the somewhat grotesque. Here too, women's education as well as some attempts to include the less privileged within the growing purview of education was very much on nationalist agendas.

What made India an exciting place to be in after the middle of the 19th century was the growing tracery of roads and railways: if the Daniells' had to hire a *budgerow* for their three-year journey through eastern and northern India, a century later they would have had the option of the train or a combination of the river, the road and the railways. It was the railways that affected an increasing number of Indians and its arrival also coincided with a world increasingly on the move – nothing unknown to animate living beings – but now at a far faster rate. By the late 19th century, there was also an interest in documenting different modes of transportation. Between 1894–96, the US-based Transportation Commission headed by railroad publicist Joseph Gladding Pangborn documented the worldwide process, backed up by an impressive portfolio of 900 images by photographer William Henry Jackson. There are elephants, camels, horses, sleds and sleighs, sedan chairs, rickshaws, railroads from Africa, Asia and Australia. From India, photographs of crowded railway platforms, a woman bowed down with a load of large tin sheets on her head, 'natives' waiting at the Madras pier – perhaps to be sent to other countries as indentured labour – circulated widely, fleeting testimonies of different life experiences.

III

Though a number of articles in this volume have appeared in *The Telegraph*, quite a few have been edited, added to and changed substantially so as to fit into the overall framework. As a result, a few may be much longer that the usual 1,200-word newspaper column. Many new visuals have been included, postcards, photographs as well as prints and a few paintings. While I have used the old names of places, except in the case of the three Presidencies, the current names have been added in parentheses. There is some repetition of people and places which might appear tedious to readers who go through all the articles; hopefully they will have the patience not to give up, keeping in mind that others might prefer the cafeteria approach – perhaps encouraged by the fact that the book is a collection of short, stand-alone pieces. A list of sources and readings that might be useful to those interested in further information has been added; however, while I've tried to track down most references, discerning readers are likely to spot a few absences. As some of the articles were written almost five years ago, I was not always as diligent as I should have been in noting down the names of authors and their work. In most instances, the marvels of the Web have helped in rectifying this shortcoming.

I would now like to meander back to my basic aspiration: that the book be read as fleeting insights into certain aspects of imperial India, not always threaded together to form a complete narrative. Though in some, the visual appears as only an illustration with little discussion around it, in quite a few articles it is more integral, and in fact, the acquisition of an unusual or exciting visual often led me on a trail of finding out more about it. And then, if I was lucky, an article was in the making. Thus, unlike most books where the visual is merely an illustration, here, in many cases, it is the *raison d'être* for a line of thinking. Visual imagery becomes the link with the past for 'after the event has ended, the picture will still exist'. It will confer on the context or place or maybe even person, 'a kind of immortality (an importance) it would otherwise never have enjoyed' (Susan Sontag). Like Sontag, I too have valorised the visual as I believe that it always has a story to tell – and sometimes that story may subvert what the text is trying to say. But this opposition is too wide a subject to go into over here – even though on occasion, in the course of this book, I might hint at an icon-text disagreement. Such is the predicament of an academic who tries to be populist!

CERIORNIS BLYTHII

'*Ceriornis Blythii*'
Lithograph based on a watercolour by John Gerrald Keulemans in
Proceedings of the Zoological Society of London, *1870*

Of Birds,
Bungalows
and
Preoccupations

27 Section.   FEMME EN GRANDE PARURE.   Livraison 13.me

'Femme en Grand Parure' (Woman in Grand Attire), in Le Hindous *series (1808–1812)*
Coloured etching by François Balthazar Solvyns

A SURVEYOR'S EYE

~~~

*W*ell before the advent of photography, the interest of visiting Western artists in the Indian way of life – its varied ethnic types, occupations, trades and so on – was reflected in sketches, drawings and, later, paintings. There was an understandable curiosity and among some, an emphasis on difference and by implication, a sense of racial superiority. Pre-eminent among the artists were the uncle-nephew team of Thomas and William Daniell and, as far as an understanding of the peoples of India was concerned, few could rival the work of the Flemish artist, François Balthazar Solvyns. He lived in Calcutta from 1791 to 1803, and his etchings and paintings of the people of Bengal, their occupations, festivals, and daily life, are quite amazing. A professional artist, Solvyns left India a disappointed man as his work was little appreciated. At around the same time, in south India, Colin Mackenzie, the first surveyor general of India, had not dissimilar interests – but in his case, he had a mandate from the East India Company. He collected hundreds of drawings, most of which are in the British Library as well as in Kolkata's Asiatic Society.

Mackenzie, a Scotsman from the Outer Hebrides, came to India in 1783 and soon became an engineer in the Madras army. However, he was an unusual army man and quickly combined military drafting, drawing and sketching with his other activities that included employing and training Indians as draftsmen, copyists and translators. Most important

Tipu Sultan's Masjid-i-ala or Jama Masjid at Seringapatnam
Photograph, c. 1920s

were the *harkaras* who, among other things, provided leads to important persons, texts and manuscripts. Orientalist blinkers apart, Mackenzie helped create a significant body of work, particularly on south India, including an extensive survey of the Nizam's dominions, documentation of the Pallava site of Mahabalipuram, temples, monuments and various occupations of the Mysore region.

This region was of great strategic significance for the British, exemplified in the defeat of Tipu Sultan in 1799. Local histories were gleaned and gathered by Mackenzie's chief Indian translator, Kavali Venkata Boriah Brahmin, known generally as Boriah. In *Illustrating India – The Early Colonial Investigations of Colin Mackenzie (1784-1821)*, Jennifer Howes discusses Boriah's role in acquiring records, getting them translated and then writing them up as 'carefully structured papers' under the overall guidance of Mackenzie. The latter wrote appreciatively of Boriah's 'more than common association of talents' that included 'a competent knowledge of several languages' and 'fidelity, accuracy and vigour of mind superior to common prejudices', all necessary for the gathering of information. The Mysore survey that concentrated on enquiries into natural history, climate, soil, medicine, disease and population also included illustrations of the people of Balla Ghaut, now identified as the region to the west of inland Karnataka. In May 1803, when Chitradurg became a significant staging post, Boriah lost no time in getting substantial information about the local population and furnishing his master with a detailed report on the local revenue system and agrarian structure. A duly impressed Mackenzie submitted the report to Governor-General Wellesley.

Together with information based on oral history, narratives and texts, draftsmen and surveyors made detailed drawings of the people of the region. Again, as was to be the case with 20th-century non-studio photography, authorial anonymity characterised many of the visuals; only one draftsman by the name of Monisse is mentioned. However, there is no lack of information on the subjects of the drawings and each of the seventy-nine included in the volume entitled *Costumes of Balla Ghaut, Carnatic, 1800-1801* has detailed captions. These describe location – both of where the visual was drawn as well as the origin of the sitter – and caste or occupation. Of particular interest is Boriah's comment that 'thus we find Mharatta (*sic*) and Canara Brahmins in Madras, Malabars (*sic*) in Ceylon, Tallungas [perhaps Telugu-speakers] in Hindostan (*sic*) [north India], and Guzaratties [Gujaratis] settled in various parts of the peninsula, distant from their original Dasoms [place of origin]'. This emphasis on geographic location remained a running theme in Mackenzie's classification, identifying people by place of origin and language as well as by caste and occupation. Such information also provides a fascinating insight into the migratory nature of the Indian population in times when physical mobility often meant walking miles through dusty paths and country roads.

Howes points out that 68 per cent of the drawings identify the caste of the sitter and also provide interesting variations in costume; for instance, although there are three drawings of '*gollas*', each person is wearing a different costume. Boriah's comment on the community is instructive – they had to 'pay a duty to government for feeding their flocks and cattle in public lands'. Rather than exclude such information from his official survey, Mackenzie encouraged his team to enrich accounts and captions with these details. In doing so he introduced a trend that combined drawings with detailed textual explanations about the people of a particular region. As surveys meant casting the net far and wide, the men encountered a range of persons during their travels, including itinerant entertainers. There is an interesting description that accompanied a drawing of high caste Brahmin girls dancing during the festival of 'Gauree or Durga'. The caption notes that while the artist could not be privy to private celebrations within the home, he was witness to the dancing beneath trees 'in this joyous season of general mirth'.

In the course of his peregrinations, Boriah collected a number of written accounts that had a direct bearing on the drawings of the people of Balla Ghaut. Apart from describing the caste system, he looked at the financial arrangements of the *raiyats* or tenant farmers. As is well known, they were vulnerable to the writ of the landlord; yet they had certain entitlements: he wrote that 'the *Coomar* or iron smith and *Badiga* or carpenter are to supply the *Ryuts* [*raiyats*] with ploughs and other instruments of husbandry without taking any price for the same'. Mackenzie seems to have done a number of drawings himself and, for three of the Madhava Guru Brahmins, a Boriah-inspired account contextualised the images appropriately. Clearly, a considerable synergy underlay the relations between Mackenzie, Boriah and the rest of the team.

In 1815–17, the Scotsman had a portrait of himself painted by Thomas Hickey, resplendent in military uniform, while three Indian pandits stood round him; in this rather fanciful representation against a backdrop of the Jain statue of Gomatesvara at Karkala (and not at Sravana Belgola as some thought), the artist has captured the difference in gaze and body language of the four men. Two men stand behind while the one at Mackenzie's left holds a palm leaf manuscript and looks expectantly in his direction. The second pandit who also holds a manuscript appears to have Mackenzie's ear and the man at the back is listening, his head slightly cocked. Tall and imperious, Mackenzie, a slight smile on his lips stands well in front of the three, much more intent on looking at the artist than in engaging with the pandits who are likely to have been important informants. Artist Thomas Hickey had carefully orchestrated the image that he was expected to create: the authoritative Englishman standing upright with three Indians, in —

for those who did not know the context – what appear to be deferential postures. The reality may of course have been different – Indian pandits were not only vital to the entire process of documentation, interpretation and translation, but also helped Mackenzie collect hundreds of palm leaf manuscripts, many of which were deposited in the Madras College Library. Mackenzie's team would have been quite lost without the likes of such men.

That visual representation was going to play a significant role in British understandings of India was clear from the 18th century onwards. Several decades later, when relations between the two countries were being violently renegotiated, the first viceroy, George Canning, got under way his ambitious *The People of India* photographic project. This eight-volume endeavour provided more technologically sophisticated visual evidence about Victoria's newly acquired subjects. However, the captions were not always as detailed as those worked on by Mackenzie and his colleagues, many of whom had spent several days with those whose likenesses they depicted. In juxtaposing the visual with the written word, the hard-working and imaginative Scotsman produced a large body of interesting material of certain intrinsic value for the future. Among other things, he provided a salience to the visual, ensuring for it a significant place in officialese for generations to come.

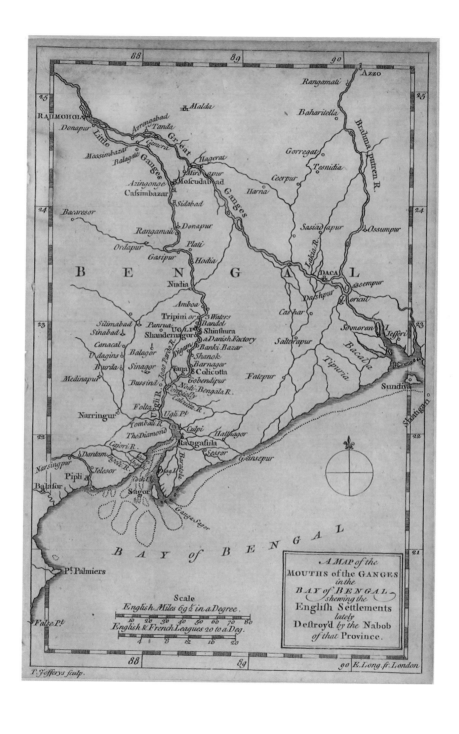

A MAP of the
MOUTHS of the GANGES
in the
BAY of BENGAL
shewing the
English Settlements
lately
Destroy'd by the Nabob
of that Province.

VISUALISING IMPERIAL
CONTROL

⟨⟨⟩

*I*n the disturbed 1850s and in the early years of Empire, when
rebellion had to be met by oppression, images based on woodcuts,
cartoons and line drawings also became partisan in the hegemonic
discourse of Empire. By this time, the visual had become essential to
governance – whether as the fingerprints and mugshots of criminals, or
maps, charts and photographs. Surveyors, cartographers, dactylographers,
engravers and even photographers and the odd artist became essential
prostheses of imperial governance. They were vital aids to British rule
committed to consolidation of authority, not only through governance
but also by an understanding of boundaries and exclusion and the
concomitant emphasis on surveillance and control. Although they were
not insignificant players within the corridors of power, little is known
about these specialists or of their work. As early as 1779, James Rennell,
a mere twenty-one-year-old army officer with a flair for surveying, was
appointed surveyor-general and undertook a comprehensive survey of the
East India Company's lands.

Left: *'Mouths of the Ganges in the Bay of Bengal, shewing the English Settlements lately
Destroy'd by the Nabob [Siraj-ud-Daulah] of that Province.'*
Map in The Gentlemen's Magazine, *London, July 1757*

Dactylography in India owed its early history to Sir William Herschel, the chief magistrate of the Hooghly district. In 1858, he first used fingerprints on native contracts, and 'with no thought toward personal identification, Herschel had Rajyadhar Konai, a local businessman, impress his hand print on a contract'. Mythology around the fingerprint has it that Konai and others were quite happy to put their palms on a contract – in an as yet largely pre-literate culture, touching the document meant as much as a signature with a quill pen. Although in 1880, the potential of fingerprints in forensic work was first put forth by Henry Faulds, in India, it was in 1897 that the governor-general in council approved a committee report which stated that fingerprints should be used for classification of criminal records.

Later that year, the Calcutta Anthropometric Bureau became the world's first Fingerprint Bureau. Two police personnel, Azizul Haque and Hem Chandra Bose, already at the Bureau, started working on the formula of Sir Edward Richard Henry, then inspector general of police, Lower Provinces, Bengal. It is a little-known fact that Henry's Method of Classification for maintaining criminal records that is still used in many English-speaking countries was, in large part, formulated by Haque and Bose under the overall direction of Henry. Researchers G.S. Sodhi and Jasjeet Kaur have noted that Henry stole all the thunder in 1900 and it was not till two decades later, and after many appeals from Haque and Bose, that the Indians were acknowledged, and characteristically, awarded honoraria and titles.

By this time, of course, the political climate had also changed substantially and in the closing years of the 19th century, the role of the visual in governance and control was firmly in place. Fingerprinting helped establish criminality while surveys and maps legitimised territory and ownership. The photograph did all this and more – its many-faceted role encompassed, at one end, mugshots, surveillance and images of oppression, and at the other, archaeological documentation, the picturesque and the beautiful. As an instrument of the age of science, it carried with it the burden of truth, of truthful representativeness. Its precursor, the lithographic print, such as this early one based on an engraving, also focussed on the pleasing and informative. It is a somewhat fanciful and not particularly well-crafted rendering of the landing point at Diamond Harbour where palm trees sway

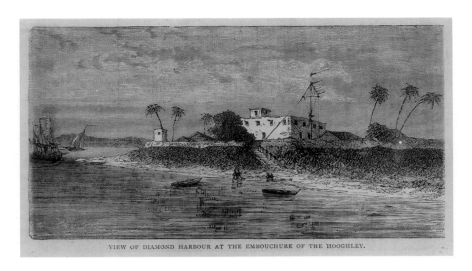

VIEW OF DIAMOND HARBOUR AT THE EMBOUCHURE OF THE HOOGHLEY.

'View of Diamond Harbour at the embouchure of the Hooghley.'
Lithograph, c. 1830s

is opposing directions. However, its details are significant – lookout point, harbour building, a couple of country boats on the river nearby while a yacht and a larger ship are further out, near the sea. It was of course the extensive and very fine work of Thomas and William Daniell that brought the print and aquatint into focus.

By the middle of the 19th century, visual discourse on Empire had evolved considerably in sophistication and technical expertise. Its appeal extended now to the satirical and ironically amusing. Cartoons – the term being coined by *Punch*, the foremost cartoon-based publication of Victorian Britain – were increasingly used, not only to lampoon a subject people, but also Anglo-Indian life. For instance, the magistrate, memsahib, clubwalla in G.P. Atkinson's *'Curry and Rice,' on forty plates. Or The Ingredients of Social Life at 'Our Station' in India* (1859) are 'the most brilliant representations of expatriate life' (Partha Mitter). Art historian Mitter goes on to point out that 'no single humorous publication made a deeper impression in India than the English comic magazine, *Punch*'. By the second half of the century, Indians had adopted the magazine's format and selective humour resulting in a range of publications such as *Delhi Sketch Book* and *The Indian Charivari* as well as local versions of *Punch* ranging from the well-known *Oudh Punch*, *Delhi Punch*, *Parsi Punch* and even the *Purneah Punch* 'from a remote town in Bengal'. These comic magazines, 'whether in Britain or in India' Mitter feels 'were an index of imperial mentality'.

In her study of vernacular versions of *Punch*, Ritu Khanduri concludes that the growing market in colonial India meant that the iconography of images had to appeal to the defenders of Empire far from home. She points out that as 'military personnel in the colonies formed a major constituency of *Punch*'s readers' the proprietors carefully nurtured this relationship. In addition, by the beginning of the 20th century, the management of *Punch* was aware of the profusion of local variants, particularly in India. Clearly this only indicated the popularity and outreach of the parent magazine. In 1902, recognising the relevance of the Indian market, one of the of proprietors, Lawrence Bradbury, set sail on a six-month world tour with 'the object chiefly of "booming" *Punch* in distant lands' (quoted in Khanduri). The cartoonist Bernard Partridge's rendering of imperial politics coincided with this visit, giving an extra ballast to Bradbury's trip. The focus of both owner and cartoonist was clearly to ensure a continued salience for *Punch* in existing as well as new colonial markets such as those in India

In this cartoon from the July 16, 1902 issue of the magazine, Britannia's left hand both encircles a Westernised version of Mother India as well as holds a trident upright. In other words, the benevolent ruler combines power with a reassuring maternal stance, confirmed by what she is saying: 'We can ill spare him: but you see we give you of our best'. Britannia waves in the direction of the army officer, who looks a bit like a younger Governor Charles Gordon of Sudan. General Gordon was besieged by the Mahdi's troops in Khartoum and killed in 1885. He immediately became a national hero, mourned publicly by hundreds. For his part, the army officer looks into the middle distance, not engaging with the two women. Thus, Britannia, symbol of the Empire, makes it a point of telling a bejewelled young woman representing India, that sacrifice and dedication to Queen and country were implicit in Britain's relationship with India. The young woman's downcast head indicated submission and obedience. Despite heavy

EASTWARD HO!

Britannia (to India). "WE CAN ILL SPARE HIM; BUT YOU SEE WE GIVE YOU OF OUR BEST!"

'Eastward Ho!'
Cartoon in Punch, July 16, 1902

odds, the strength of the armed forces are there to take charge, a resplendent Britannia seems to say, her plumed helmet and chest armour indicating female power. In the land of the mother goddess, Partridge obviously felt that such imagery would go down well, not only with the rulers but also with Indian readers of *Punch*. In addition, it would have a particular appeal to the armed forces, shoring up once more their influence and strength after 1857.

By the time Partridge's cartoons reached India, Viceroy Curzon had decided on the Partition of Bengal, and the shift of the capital from Calcutta to New Delhi was on the cards. Many administrative and legislative changes were to follow and Indian nationalist politics was to come of age with the return from South Africa of Mohandas Karamchand Gandhi; in this fast-changing world where the substance of politics and authority was to be increasingly interrogated, visual imagery of the ironic, descriptive or merely pleasing, had a growing role to play. It was also the time when photojournalism gained early credibility, ensuring a respectable space for the visual in public discourse.

SPOOKY FOR ALL TIMES

◀━━✦

For the British rulers, whose morbidity and mortality rates were alarmingly high in an inhospitable land, trying to build homes and offices that minimised the ravages of disease and discomfort was by no means a minor preoccupation. As early as the end of the 18th century, the bungalow emerged as a distinct meld of styles. The *Hobson-Jobson* – that invaluable lexicon on legitimate and other entrants into Queen's English – has a long and detailed description of it, the etymology of the word being traced back to the common hut of the Bengal (*Bangla*) peasant. By the end of the 18th century, the East India Company's engineering department was working on transforming the *bangla*, now also known as bungelow, bungelo, bangalla and, finally, bungalow.

Though initially the term referred to dwellings in upcountry Bengal, Anthony King, an authority on the bungalow, found mentions of it in 1810 Lucknow, Bombay and parts of south India. After 1820, notes King, when the term 'bungalow' came to stay, the semantic change coincided with a widening of its meaning: it was now not limited only to an Indian-type dwelling but also included those made of bricks and mortar – and later, with a flat, terraced roof rather than only a sloping one. The latter developed into official dwellings for those who were to run the Raj and with the establishment of the Public Works Board in 1854, a Military-Board style of architecture emerged.

Tea planter's bungalow on a high plinth with wide enveloping veranda, north Bengal
Photograph, c. 1940s

The gallery round the *bangla* was later developed into the all-important veranda. In 1793, the artist William Hodges observed that rooms radiated outwards from the central space, and verandas were often partitioned off to accommodate servants and others. This feature of tropical architecture possibly came to India from Portugal. Though variants started proliferating in urban areas, the bungalow had a distinctly *moffusil* air about it. Unlike the courtyard-based homes of the urban 'native' quarters where the focus was inwards, the bungalows looked outwards, to the veranda, well-tended gardens and the compound beyond.

The word 'compound' can be traced to *kampungs* of the British factories in Malaya; the concept soon spread to other parts of the Empire, encapsulating fields and in the case of bungalows, their often extensive gardens, usually enclosed by what was known as the 'compound wall'. Writing of the commissioner's residence in Cuttack, R.C. Dutt, an early member of the Indian Civil Service (ICS), commented that the 'park-like compound with its avenues and grassy lawns and shady trees' gave shelter to over twenty deer. Notions of boundary and inclusion secured life for the privileged; walls and compounds became the markers of belonging and of exclusion.

Of abiding interest – and not without an air of mystery – were the bungalows for the itinerant in the *moffusils*: the sub-divisional officer on duty, the engineer on inspection and the forester out to trap poachers. Thus, irrigation, canal, forest and the generic inspection bungalows catered to these specialised personnel. The circuit houses were for the judiciary while the *dak* bungalow acquired a certain ubiquity – and, as we shall see, notoriety. Taken over from the Moghuls, the *dak* system relied on relays of runners who carried the mail. *Dak* bungalows marked the point where relays changed, and also where officers and other travellers could rest for the night. For inexplicable reasons, these rather basic and often uncomfortable abodes excited the imagination of the likes of traveller-informant Francis Younghusband, ICS-wallah John Beames and creative writers from Rudyard Kipling to Satyajit Ray.

In the absence of anything but tents, and maybe even the open sky, they were indispensable to many and not only those on official duty – wayfarers, Younghusband on his several trips – acknowledged or secret – or the homeless traveller in search of salvation. Deep verandas with ancient planter's or deck chairs, old trees in the compound, a tattered but fascinating visitor's book and the decrepit *khansama*, that general dogsbody whose watery *matan ishtoo*, no match for his cornucopia of anecdotes and fairytales, were essential components of the *mise en scène*. Culinary finesse or the lack of it depended upon the *khansama*'s virtuosity, age and mood. While the assured entry of crème caramel for dessert earned it the sobriquet of '365', a few were lucky to be treated to fine Mughlai cuisine prepared by the last survivor in a line of Muslim *khansamas*. More often, if one was fortunate, a passable Country Captain chicken appeared within minutes of the disappearance of a squawking bird, its 'sudden death' more than apocryphal. Or if one was not that fortunate, one would have to stomach dished up 'fowls [that] lay the eggs of finches, but develop the bones of vultures'. So wrote a frustrated *dak* bungalow inmate in that other institution of the *dak* bungalow, the much-thumbed visitor's book (quoted in Bhandari). In his account of Kashmir, Younghusband provides details on what to expect in *dak* bungalows situated at every 14 miles: 'for the payment of one rupee a furnished room is provided and on further payment meals may be obtained at any time but "bedding" must always be taken, as nothing but the bare bed is provided.'

Nicer *dak* and forest bungalows were usually situated on the banks of pristine streams, amidst deep forests or on hilltops. Even then, often, sylvan daytime surroundings were quickly transformed into the eerie and insecure when, with nightfall, the jungle's brooding presence seemed a little too close for comfort, a howling wind keening like a wayward banshee. Nor was it difficult to mistake the hollow cough of the *chowkidar* for that of an ambitious panther or see the coils of a hamadryad in the dim half-light of a dying candle. Who would argue that the gnarled branches of the *peepul* or *neem* swaying in the breeze on a full-moon midsummer's night did not harbour the shreds of a makeshift noose? Particularly if one's by-the-wavering-light-of-the-kerosene-lantern bedtime reading had been of a selective nature. Rajika Bhandari reminds one of the chequered history of many a *dak* bungalow during the 19th century when cholera, malaria and other deadly fevers carried off many. Often when travellers fell ill far away from home, the *dak* bungalow was their only refuge – and it was not unusual for some to be found dead the following morning. Rudyard Kipling added darkly, that in the days that men drove from Calcutta to the Northwest, some of the *dak* bungalows along the Grand Trunk Road had 'handy little cemeteries in their compounds'. Indeed stark testimony to long days and rough rides! His wry comment on the *dak* bungalow ghost is instructive: 'A ghost that would voluntarily hang about a *dak*-bungalow would be mad of course'. Yet as so many close to madness had indeed died in these places 'there must be a fair percentage of lunatic ghosts'.

In 'My Own True Ghost Story', Kipling writes of these 'objectionable places to put up in' where *khansamas* were as old as the bungalows and often 'an excited snake' was on the threshold to welcome the weary traveller. Hardly surprising that one such bungalow – and Kipling had lived in many, it being his 'business' to do so – is the locale for a spine-chilling ghost story; until, of course, the denouement. Scampering rats are the culprits, enticing a fervid brain to think of billiard balls, if not cannons, in the next room

An inspection bungalow, United Provinces. Photograph, c. 1930s

separated from his by a flimsy partition. Many decades later, Satyajit Ray noted that 'if a place is spooky – and dak bungalows have a reputation of being so – it will be so at all times'. Thus in 'The Indigo Terror' (or '*Neel atanko*'), he found the *dak* bungalow, with its charpoy and chair with only one arm intact, a suitable venue for the tragic end of an indigo planter who had shot his dog and then himself a hundred years ago. His restless spirit finds refuge in the protagonist, and so the tale proceeds.

Interestingly, successive post-Independence governments have seen fit to leave the musty old official British bungalow strictly alone, spookiness and all. The ramshackle *dak* bungalow, the eerie forest rest house, where wild animals nudge hopefully at creaky bathroom doors, or the stately Lutyensesque residence in the country's capital are testimonies to the Raj's eclectic architectural career. Cities and roads have been renamed, railways and the armed forces modernised, but railway colonies, stations and cantonments retain their basic colonial architecture, layout and design.

'Views taken from Col. Young's Bungalow at Mussorie in the Himalayas'
Watercolour by Emily Eden, c. 1840s

'GOING TO THE HILLS'

*The 1850s was clearly a decade of vast change in India; it saw the coming of the railways, telegraph and change in governance offset by rumour and rebellion, greased cartridges, dubious chapattis and indigenous rage. In the summer of 1857, Debendranath Tagore found himself almost trapped in Simla (Shimla). There were rumours of Gurkhas on the rampage ... and Meerut suddenly seemed quite near. In *Swarachita Jiban-Charit* (*Autobiography*), which deals at length with his Himalayan sojourn, Debendranath is quite candid on why he left home so often: it was not only wanderlust but also an urge to escape the expectations of indigent and debt-ridden relatives. His wife Sharada remained in Calcutta, coping with a growing brood of children and increasing family responsibilities while he was free to roam in the Himalaya. In 1873, Debendranath took his youngest son, Rabindranath, on an extended mountain holiday as well.

Although Simla was to become the summer capital of the Raj in 1864, there was, by the 1850s, a substantial administrative presence in the town, including the ubiquitous Bengali clerk, lawyer and teacher. A few quickly befriended the scion of the Tagore family, asking him to join them when they decided to flee from Simla. Declining their offer, Debendranath decided to move more into the interior. However, this was easier said than done as coolies were no longer available. Finally, a ferocious-looking coolie *sardar* provided him with the men, and Debendranath set off for the safety

A lady in a dandi, *Bhowali, Kumaon, United Provinces. Photograph, c. 1930s*

of Dagshahi, a cantonment also known for its sanatorium. After hearing that things were calmer, he returned to Simla, only to decide on another trek, this time in the direction of the 'native' states of Rampur and Bhajji. He was at peace walking, riding and being carried in a *jhampan* (more comfortable than a *dandi*) through dense jungles, living in remote villages, occasionally in *dak* bungalows, otherwise in the open, eating coarse chapattis made of *makke ki atta* mixed with *atta,* drinking milk and tea. And soon he sighted the mighty Satadru (Sutlej) far below, 'glistening like a silver leaf in the sunlight'. For one of the founders of the Brahmo Samaj, the solitude of the mountains gave time and space for meditation. Debendranath was quite the exception, as there were not many spiritual explorers like him who wrote about their experiences till much later. Some years into the 20th century, Rabindranath, who had been deeply influenced by his first visit to the mountains with his otherwise remote father, went to Ramgarh in Kumaon. Mahadevi Verma too lived in what was then a small hamlet for several summers. In recent years, her home has been converted into a library.

But this was several decades later, when hill stations had become a part of the everyday vocabulary of Indians as well. When Debendranath decided to spend time in Simla, the hill station as a place of leisure and respite – and of course some surveillance – was the preserve of the ruling class. Historian Dane Kennedy likens them to 'sentinels over heat-shimmering plains ... curious monuments to the colonial presence'. It is not clear why Kennedy felt that hill stations were a bit of a curiosity, as certainly in India, their continued if not growing attraction long after Independence would indicate otherwise. The phrase 'going to the hills' has been enthusiastically adopted by Indian middle-class travellers, there being different 'seasons' for Bengalis, Gujaratis, Tamilians and so on. While the top favourites remain Shimla, Mussoorie, Nainital, Darjeeling, Ootacamund and Mahabaleshwar, there are many others. Some are less known today although they had been very popular over a century ago. A number started out as sanatoriums and health resorts not only for patients of tuberculosis but also for others weary and sick from living in the fetid plains.

Most major hill stations were founded in the 1840s and 1850s. Relentless Indian summers, mosquito bites that became 'huge blisters' and the fear of cholera, typhoid and the likes provided ample grist for nightmares and hastened the search for escape routes. While men would go up for short spells, families stayed on for months. Flora Annie Steel, that astute commentator on life in India for the memsahib, felt that despite the separation dreaded by wives (one never knew which lissome wench in the servants' quarters the sahib would train his eye on), a summer in the hills would ultimately pay off. Often, missionary settlements were responsible for interest in a particular area. In 1850, on a visit to Almora in Kumaon, Reverend John Henry Budden of the Mirzapur Mission of the London Missionary Society was asked by Captain (later Sir Henry) Ramsay to start a mission in the area. The society agreed and two buildings adjoining the bazaar – formerly a mess-room and a billiard room for the regimental officers –were taken over for mission work with one of the buildings being used as the mission chapel. Sunday services were offered in both Hindustani and English: clearly, the antecedents of the building were not delved into too closely. Soon Almora grew into much more than a missionary base.

If it became a centre of retreat for survey, telegraph and railway staff, Mussooree (Mussoorie) attracted subalterns out for a good time, and of course, Simla was jealously guarded by top military and civilian personnel. It was the world of the Kiplingesque Mrs Hauksbee or even Phil Garron who 'went native' by marrying Dunmaya. It provided a brief spring for rakish officers, vampish women, subterfuge and fantasy. While some remained isolated barracks —such as Chakrata and Jalapahar — others clearly became thriving social and educational centres. Treks, hikes and more serious mountaineering, birding, fishing and *shikar* were to be looked forward to in the long summer months.

Educational institutions flourished and children lucky enough not to be sent home to school and a soulless existence during holidays with elderly relatives studied in the growing number of boarding schools often run by missionaries and the Catholic Church. The racial divide was strictly maintained and the *babalog* were warned against befriending their Indian peers. Yet a certain interdependence was inevitable. Kennedy draws attention to the fact that as 'most hill stations were economically parasitical', they depended heavily on state support as well as on private investment. Even those that did not become part of official India flourished once they became municipalities. Simla was clearly privileged, as beginning with Governor-General Auckland's 1837 momentous visit that had involved a retinue of 12,000, successive governments ended spending considerable time there than in Calcutta, the capital till 1911. At the regional level too, hill stations were acquired by various provincial governments, ensuring a secure existence for areas that might otherwise have lapsed into poverty – or not grown at all.

As officialdom and social life picked up in these select enclaves, precursors of new age developers had a field day; palatial buildings as well as more modest summer homes, malls, bandstands and theatres proliferated – and so did the need to record the India that was not only heat and dust for those back home. Before the arrival of the camera, in 1788, the Daniell uncle-and-nephew team had visited Garhwal. They were the first European artists to record the Himalaya, although a volume exclusively on the region had to wait till 1836 when Lt George White's richly illustrated notes on

GENERAL VIEW OF SIMLA, TAKEN FROM JAKO HILL.

'General View of Simla, taken from Jako Hill.'
Lithograph based on an 1865 photograph by Samuel Bourne

his tours, *Simla and Mussooree, Himalayan Mountains*, was published. And of course, there were Emily Eden, Alicia Eliza Scott, Charlotte Canning and a host of others who painted mainly for pleasure. With the appearance of photography, availability and modes of representation changed radically. Photographer Samuel Bourne, not only set up a studio in Simla in 1863, but also found it a convenient base for his treks. His portfolio that included many generic hill station shots – the snow-clad Christ Church in Simla (1863), Church of St. John-in-the Wilderness in Naini Tal (1866), of Bhim Tal (1866) on calm mornings, of clubs, gubernatorial residences and even monuments and temples served colonial memories well and put the Indian hill station firmly on the map. This print of Jako Hill, a popular tourist spot in Simla is based on one of Bourne's panoramic shots. English-style cottages with familiar names were built and acquired, as the re-creation of nostalgic ambiences was a significant mnemonic ploy. 'Our spirit soars as we read of the "Eagle's Nest", "The Crags" or "The Highlands" whilst "Sunny Bank" and "The Dovecote" opens up a vista of quiet restfulness', wrote the eloquent Flora Annie Steel and Grace Gardiner.

Debendranath obviously wrote about his journeys after he returned to Calcutta. He carried neither pen nor paper with him – nor, for that matter, did Samuel Bourne, who nevertheless wrote several despatches for *British Journal of Photography* between 1863 and 1870. These are fascinating accounts of an intrepid, though somewhat rapacious, adventurer engaged in bringing home several portfolios of India's landscape. He wrote, 'Before I commenced photography I did not see half the beauties of nature that I see now, and the glory and power of a precious landscape has often passed before me and left but a feeble impression on my untutored mind; but it will never be so again.' When, at the end of ten weeks, he headed back for Simla, 'scattered over with pleasant bungalows, the abodes of comfort and civilisation', Bourne was grateful that he had 147 negatives 'of scenery [that had] never been photographed before', and that none of his precious equipment nor his glass plates had been damaged. Over the decades, the Himalaya have been photographed, filmed, digitalised and hill stations have been Indianised with properties changing hands, *chawls* and seedy hotels replacing elegant theatres and old establishments. Yet, the experience of 'going to the hills' – immortalised visually by Bourne and others – flourishes; the entrepreneurial spirit of several tour operators and enterprising vendors of adventure have ensured that for generations to come.

FLOWER POWER

*A*n integral part of the imperial process was to keep up a constant flow of information on life in the colonies for those who stayed behind. The colonial penchant for collecting, cataloguing and reporting found great opportunities in alien lands. Material objects of all kinds – toys, masks, books, manuscripts, paintings, stuffed animals and birds soon made their way to homes in Britain. And for the more adventurous, caches of plants, seeds and specimens from exotic India were carefully carried back. Horticulturists, plant explorers and commercial exporters of flora entered the scene, providing a different and little known angle to British imperialism. The import of flora for individual collectors, and of course, for the Royal Botanic Gardens at Kew spawned a mini industry in appropriate plant boxes and containers for delicate plants that had to be carted by porters many hundreds of miles over difficult terrains. Irate ship captains begrudged the space taken by their unusual cargo that required some care such as protection from livestock with whom they usually travelled (Eugenia Herbert).

Soon, garden styles and designs became a part of colonialism's expanding discourse and process of acquisition. If daisies, daffodils, peonies and hydrangeas came to inhabit Indian gardens, brought by those longing for a bit of home in alien lands, the reverse too was true. However, many of these migrants predated imperialism, and were 'nativised' over the centuries.

Though what Lucile Brockway has called 'botanical imperialism' had roots in the Middle Ages, European imperial expansion helped greatly in the cultivation of exotics at home. For those who could not travel, explore and experience at first hand, the landscapes of the Other, the import of exotics was 'as important in shaping the imaginative geographies of British imperialism as exploration and travel abroad' (Rebecca Preston). Descriptions of exotics cultivated in conservatories that imitated Indian pleasure pavilions all but transported their owners to the land of their origin: a particularly amusing 1831 account of the sensuous hallucinogenic, the *datura* in the *Gardener's Magazine* (edited by John Claudius Loudon), led the correspondent to comment that 'the delicate whiteness of its large pendulous bells, contrasted with its ample green foliage, and as viewed in the imperfect illumination of candlelight, made a grand and exhilarating spectacle, one that seemed to us Orientally luxurious'. One admirer of this grand flower was even moved to quote Virgil as he threw himself into a spacious armchair.

At the same time, there was a subtle resistance growing and Preston quotes *The Gentlewoman's Book of Gardening* (1892) that refused entry to the hyacinth – a relative of the English bluebell because 'its smell is not an English one – it is too rich and heavy'. It went on rather prudishly to comment that 'it breathe [*sic*] reminiscences of its Eastern home, and we associate it more readily with the song of the bulbul ... It is one of the harem of night flowers'. Though the book protested 'against this terrible invasion of foreigners' like the dahlia, abutilon, gladioli and begonia, these soon became staples of the English cottage garden and its heirs in India. From the middle of the 19th century, as mental travelling or Mesmerism, as it was called, reached almost 'epic proportions in the popular imagination' (Preston), it hardly required a visit to the tropics for many an avid gardener to become familiar with unknown terrains. The English country garden that now became host to exotics allowed a private – if somewhat specialised – understanding of Empire. Suitably orientalised garden architecture provided the look and feel of the 'torrid zones'. There was, however, an important difference: built-up specialised spaces – very important in the overall structure of the Islamic garden – were harmoniously blended into the landscape. This was quite unlike many British gardens designed by specialists like Scottish

4463.

Fitch, del et lith.

R. F. & R. imp.

Yellow Abutilon
Hand-coloured botanical illustration, c. 1870s

Cow parsley, foliage and ears of wheat
Lithograph, c. 1870s

botanist John Claudius Loudon who could somewhat dishonestly suggest to a credulous gentry that palms set in 'a glazed Mosque, Pyramid or Pagoda, … might give a pretty good idea of the scenery of the torrid zone'.

Not unexpectedly, in time a nationalistic reaction grew, and by the last years of the 19th century, gardeners, many of them women, started working on the Old English garden; some even experimented with the Shakespearean. Garden books, journals and nurseries proliferated and as Eugenia Herbert has commented, 'at times, gardening took on attributes of a blood sport' with various exponents of different schools putting forth their points of view. The mid-century style of neat beds was quickly displaced by Gertude Jekyll's 'naturalism' that experimented with the wild garden where hardy perennials, grasses and rock gardens combined natives with exotics that could survive without coddling. At the same time, there was also the influential view that the overpowering influence of the mysterious East had to be kept at bay in the garden, if not in real life. It could be there, argued gardener Barbara Campbell, as a mere hint as otherwise, if 'allowed to dominate, it [oriental suggestion] becomes incongruous, and would denationalise the garden'. Xenophobia came in many forms, and it was all very well to be seduced by the single *datura* on an intoxicated evening: to be surrounded by many others of its kind would be overwhelming – and might even threaten a very different garden style.

Thus, it was equally important to grow 'English' flowers, so as to 'remind one of home' (Lady Beatrix Stanley quoted in Herbert). In her study of flowers that would grow in India, Lady Stanley concluded that while zinnias, coreopsis, phlox and petunias did well in the south, 'roses are no use in Madras'. On the other hand, in Delhi, they could compete with the best in England. And the further north one went, the easier it was to grow good roses. In 1916, Lady Rosamund Lawrence, wife of civil servant Henry Lawrence, wrote of the bunches of roses that she sent to the matron at Dufferin Hospital in Karachi. In summer, cottages in the hill stations were awash with the cheerful abandon of climbing roses while the tea and standard varieties were more strictly monitored and pruned. At the same time, many realised that it would be short-sighted to ignore the hardy natives in the many bungalows and compounds of British India. In spite of her longing for the flowers of home, Beatrix Stanley admitted that unless one grew the indigenes, 'one misses many lovely and interesting plants'. Yet, it would not do to forget that the manicured garden within compound walls served to maintain identity in a racially and class divided society. Like the much-loved culinary variants of curries, mulligatawnies, fish molee and that soft, rice-based invalid-cum-nursery Bengali comfort food, *pish-pash*, such gardens ended up increasingly as creoles (Herbert), not quite Indian and not quite English or even European.

Serious forays into large-scale visions of Oriental flora had to be reserved for visits to, for instance, the Royal Botanic Gardens at Kew. At the institutional level, by 1880, its director was to describe the Royal Botanic Gardens as one in which 'a vast assemblage of plants from every accessible part of the Earth's surface is systematically cultivated'. Two men greatly influential in the growth of Kew were the father-son team of the botanist, Sir William Hooker, and his son, Joseph. Sir William's personal collection of dried plants was the basis for Kew's Herbarium, while his son, Joseph, specialised in living flora. He visited India between 1847 and 1851, and apart from gathering material to write his seven-volume opus, *Flora of British India*, Joseph Hooker carried back thirty new species of the Himalayan rhododendron for the Royal Botanic Gardens. His *Rhododendrons of Sikkim-Himalaya* with lavish illustrations by botanical artist Walter Hood Fitch, soon whetted the appetite of English gardeners in search of the exotic. They were further encouraged by Hooker's revelation that these seemed to grow better in the Cornish Riviera than in Sikkim. The hardy bushes were soon to find their way into private gardens, and till today, the beautiful golden rhododendron, rarely seen in Indian gardens, coexists with the English rose in cottage gardens, reminding us that many plants are unwitting bearers of an unusual colonial legacy.

A MISSIONARY'S
PASSION

ittle is recorded and perhaps known of the other lives of William Carey, a founder of the Baptist Missionary Society; it is an established fact that he had the Bible translated into Bengali, Sanskrit and several dialects, and that educational institutions have been named after him. However, it is not much known that he was a horticultural expert. Or that he was married three times, and was hardly a caring husband and father. His first wife, Dorothy, an unlettered young girl from rural England, was driven insane by the move to a totally alien environment and of being trapped in a seemingly loveless marriage; there was also evidence of his four sons being somewhat neglected. Carey's private collection of botanical specimens was second only to that of the East India Company's Botanic Gardens at Calcutta. Though he had wanted to work in Tahiti or West Africa, when he found himself in Bengal in 1793, he wasted little time in nurturing his passion for the local flora, planting, organising and cataloguing. Clearly, Carey also 'wasted' little time on his family and, while marvelling at his friend's intellectual devotion, his colleague, Joshua Marshman, could not but add 'an insane wife, frequently wrought up to a state of most distressing excitement, was in the next room'. Sympathetic friends felt that Carey did not know how to cope with the situation; or is it

William Carey
Lithograph, c. 1840s

that he would rather spend his time in intellectual and horticultural pursuits, leaving the unfortunate Dorothy to fend for herself?

In his five-acre garden in Serampore, Carey had created a private botanical garden complete with aviaries, four enormous tanks for aquatic flora and thousands of plants from humble grasses to mahogany trees. Not everyone understood his passion, and when Marshman chided him for not wearing a wide-brimmed hat while he worked in his garden, Carey apparently retorted, 'What does Marshman know about a garden? He only appreciates it, as an ox

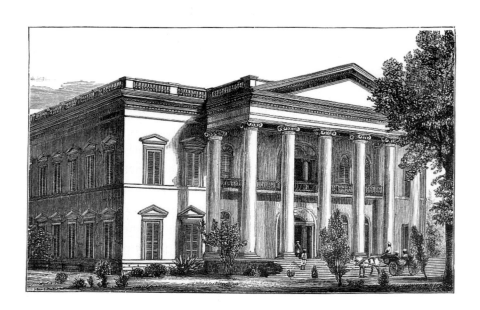

Serampore College. Lithograph, c. 1850s

MEMORIES OF BELONGING

does grass!' He soon became a close friend and associate of the legendary William Roxburgh, the head of the Calcutta Botanic Gardens, consulting him frequently on scientific names and other details. In 1798, Carey noted with some irritation that 'the saul tree, which, being an unnamed genus, Dr. Roxburgh, as a mark of respect to me, has called *Careya saulea*'. In part his objection arose from the fact that he did not think that European names should be used for indigenous plants. Though Carey's view hardly prevailed in botanical taxonomy, the *sal* came to be known as the *Shorea robusta*, and Roxburgh named instead another deciduous tree of eastern India, the *kumbhi* or slow match tree, *Careya Arborea*. While in Burma (Myanmar) its wood is used for the construction of house posts and furniture, in India, a variety of silkworms is fed on its leaves.

A few years after coming to India, Carey wrote to friends and associates in England that he was 'sending an assortment of Hindoo gods to the British Museum, and some other curiosities to different friends'. In return, 'Do send a few tulips, daffodils, snowdrops, lilies, and seeds of other things'. He wistfully added that even weeds and thistles were welcome – provided they were English. The person who was to bring this precious cargo by sea was instructed not to put it in the hold; rather, 'send the roots in a net or basket, to be hung up anywhere out of the reach of salt water, and the seeds in a separate small box. You need not be at any expense, any friend will supply these things. The cowslips and daisies of your fields would be great acquisitions here'. Carey had to wait another twenty years before memorabilia from the English countryside arrived at his doorstep in 1821, complete with sods of earth: his delight was unbounded and he wrote, 'That I might be sure not to lose any part of your valuable present, I shook the bag over a patch of earth in a shady place: on visiting which a few days afterwards I found springing up, to my inexpressible delight, a *Bellis perennis* of our English pastures. I know not that I ever enjoyed, since leaving Europe, a simple pleasure so exquisite as the sight of this English Daisy afforded me; not having seen one for upwards of thirty years, and never expecting to see one again' (quoted in Ray Desmond). However, another keen naturalist, Lady Sarah Amherst, wife of Governor-General William Amherst, found Carey's nostalgia somewhat cloying; she felt that he was being a bit foolhardy in attempting to grow plants in a 'climate nature never intended them for'. She was being more than a little short-sighted as soon exotics were to populate the English garden, challenging the argument of the limitations of climates and the overall environment.

In spite of Lady Amherst's criticism of his 'misguided passion' (Herbert) for English flowers, Carey set up a system of exchange with well-known botanists in other parts of the world and soon became an acknowledged expert, giving frequent lectures and advice. A keen observer of wildlife and fauna as well, Carey recorded all that he saw in his garden in great detail: in 1796 he wrote, 'We have sparrows and water-wagtails, one species of crow, ducks, geese, and common fowls; pigeons, teal, ortolans, plovers, snipes like those in Europe; but others, entirely unlike European birds, would fill a volume'. Insects too were very numerous, and 'I have seen about twelve sorts of grylli, or grasshoppers and cricket', eight or ten sorts of ants, including termites who 'will eat through an oak chest in a day or two and devour all its contents'. Butterflies, however, were not as numerous. While fish and rice were the staple diet of the Bengalis, for his own consumption Carey found that 'edible vegetables are scarce, and fruit far from plentiful. You will perhaps wonder at our eating many things here which no one eats in England': three or four sorts of arum, poppy leaves, amaranths, pumpkins, gourds, calabashes, and the egg-plant.

The realisation that there was a need to institutionalise and share the information being gathered led Carey and Marshman to set up, in 1820, the Agricultural and Horticultural Society of India. A decade later, Dwarkanath Tagore, grandfather of Rabindranath, became a member of the society. The founders particularly wanted Indians to become members and were gratified that, apart from them, at the first meeting, there were only three other Europeans present. In true missionary spirit, in his twelve-page introduction to Roxburgh's *Hortus Bengalensis, or a Catalogue of the Plants Growing in the Honourable East India Company's Botanic Gardens at Calcutta*, Carey urged English residents all over India to set apart a small plot in their gardens for local plants whose native names they could glean from their servants. In fact, the majority of the many indigenous plants cultivated in the Botanic Gardens had been acquired through contributions from such persons. The

'*Erythyrina Arborescens*'
Hand-coloured illustration in Flora Indica 3 *by William Roxburgh, 1932*

society provided valuable information on how to enhance the quality of soil, cropping methods, the introduction of new and useful plants as well as on improvements in livestock and farm implements.

A message from the good padre for the imperial rulers was not long in coming: with improved agricultural practices, the surplus of grain could be exported, and this, besides 'her opium, her indigo, her silk, and her cotton' would greatly tend to enrich India and endear Britain to her. The society continues today in Calcutta as the Agri-Horticultural Society of India, its founder commemorated in a bust installed in the Metcalfe Hall in 1842, by another of Carey's eminent botanist friends, Nathaniel Wallich. In 1823, a critically ill William Carey – in bed with a fever following a dislocation of the hip-joint – watched as the fury of the Hooghly River in spate washed away his botanic treasures or buried them under sand. As soon as it was possible, he was carried to view the scene of desolation: his collection was gone and his careful scientific arrangement of orders and families had been washed away. Though deeply saddened, within the hour, Carey was writing off for new specimens and in a few years 'the place [became] as lovely if not so precious, as before'. He enjoyed his garden and his research for another decade and when the septuagenarian William Carey, known popularly as 'the Father of Modern Missions', died in 1834, his third wife, Grace was by his side.

EARLY BIRDERS

⌒⌒

*F*rom the 1850s onwards, commercial uses of the camera and the proliferation of photographic studios became increasingly popular. However, other forms of visual representation also continued to be indispensable. Apart from the more covert activities of Empire through police and military, the growth of the colonial disciplines of anthropology, ethnography, archaeology and so on found imagery most useful. In the early years, detailed drawings and lithographs were used extensively, and often, individual artists with nothing more than pecuniary interests in mind became pioneers of a style that lent itself easily to professional use and analysis. A few artist-travellers like Tilly Kettle, William Hodges, Johann Zoffany, François Solvyns, Thomas Daniell and his nephew, William, produced impressive folios, many of their visual depictions providing insights into the country's geographic and ecological diversity, and architectural sites as well as into Indian society, occupations and customs.

In some cases, work by established artists accompanied written accounts, impressive precursors of today's travelogues. Such travellers were not only tourists but also missionaries, military men, engineers, doctors and government officers, who had a keen interest in recording the environment of an alien, if not intimidating and fascinating, land. For instance, the lithograph of 'The Adjutant' reproduced here is part of a set of twenty-two original drawings that William Daniell had done to accompany a descriptive

THE ADJUTANT.

'The Adjutant.'
Lithograph based on a drawing by William Daniell and engraved by R.Brandard, c. 1790s

volume by John Hobart Caunter. Caunter had come to India as a cadet and after returning to England, became a chaplain to the Earl of Thanet. *The Oriental Annual, or, Scenes in India* published in 1836 is an account of this young man's travels in the country. Apart from vivid descriptions of his sea voyage, the infamous high surf at Madras harbour, and inland journeys to Madurai and Tanjore in the south, Caunter was also a keen observer of nature. It is likely that during his journeys – on which the younger Daniell accompanied him with the express mandate of acting as visual recorder –

the author saw many birds and was able to identify a few; ornithology as a science had just about arrived in India as by 1820, using the binomial nomenclature of the Swedish botanist, Carl Linnaeus (1707–1778), birds started being classified.

For the benefit of 'the mere English reader' who was unfamiliar with the bird, Caunter described the adjutant stork – 'a bird of the crane kind very common in India' – in great (and somewhat fanciful) detail. He had seen several on the banks of the Balliapatam (Vallapatanam) River that flows through present-day Kerala and Karnataka. It was almost five feet tall with a wingspan of fifteen feet. 'The bill,' he wrote, 'which opens far back into the head, is so vast a size, that it will readily enclose a full-grown goose: it is near three feet long. The head and neck of this bird are bare, but deformed by small spongy excrescences like warts, and thin patches of strong curly hair. A long pouch hangs from the bottom of the neck over the breast, thinly covered with a short feathery growth, and terminated by a tuft of long hair resembling a stunted tail'. The author felt that the bird had acquired its common name from the fact of 'the singular circumstance of its appearing at a distance like a person in military undress, which in India consists of a white jacket and trousers'. He felt that adjutant storks were truly the scavengers of watercourses, devouring whatever they could find. However, they had a special status among the Hindus who believed 'that the souls of Adjutants are possessed by the souls of Brahmins; shooting them, therefore, they consider an act of unpardonable wickedness'. Caunter's account is a close approximation to the adjutant stork as described in modern-day field guides to Indian birds; a tribute not only to his powers of observation but also to Daniell's capacity to reproduce visually the bird, its distinctive features as well as its domain of mangrove and water. Caunter describes at some length the mangrove tree whose sturdy roots were covered with oysters: 'it is no uncommon thing for the crew of boats gather from these strange beds a generous meal of those crustaceous luxuries'.

Caunter and Daniell belonged to the tradition of observers who felt that it was their duty to present a 'true' account of India to those back home. This growing emphasis on realism was a reflection of the evolution of positivistic enquiry and a movement away from romanticism: ecstasy at the

'Yellow-billed blue magpie'
Hand-coloured illustration in Birds of Asia, Vol. III *by John Gould, 1861–66*

sublime was giving way to a pragmatic approach to the universe and a belief in the laws that governed it. By the early decades of the 19th century, the Asiatic Society of Bengal that had been set up in 1784 by Sir William Jones, the Sanskritist and lawyer, had an important role to play in the growth of systematic enquiry in India, including ornithology. Some years later, there were others like ornithologist and artist John Gould whose several volumes of *Birds of Asia* were a substantial contribution to this growing area of interest. Quite often his sketches were worked on and painted by the young Edward Lear while Gould's wife, Elizabeth also finished and coloured them in, as well as made lithographs for reproduction. Lear painted these long before he visited India and produced over 2,000 drawings from his trip. It was later that he became a noted creator of nonsense verse.

Edward Blyth, who was recruited as curator of the Asiatic Society's museum in Calcutta in 1841, had a passion for natural history, much of it in the area of ornithology and entomology. For over twenty years, he published many descriptions of new species – while drawing a pittance for a salary. He became Allan Octavian Hume's mentor, a man generally well known in history for his role in Indian nationalist politics. Hume was deeply interested in education and theosophy – but was a proficient ornithologist as well. In 1849, he was posted to the Bengal cadre of the ICS and combined his duties as magistrate and later commissioner with a great interest in education for rural youth, agricultural reform, conservation of forests, and of course, birds. Known variously as 'the Father of Indian ornithology' or as 'the Pope of Indian ornithology' by those who found him too dogmatic, Hume pursued his interest with an almost missionary zeal, believing that 'the study of Natural History in all its branches offers, next to religion, the most powerful safeguard against those worldly temptations to which all ages are exposed'.

In his spare time (such as it was), Hume studied the birds of the Indian subcontinent, and spent about £20,000 of his own money – a huge sum in those days – in establishing the largest ornithological museum and library of the time in his home, Rothney Castle at Jako Hill, Simla. It consisted of 63,000 bird skins and 19,000 eggs. He had planned to write a definitive book on the birds of India based on his voluminous notes, but in 1884, while

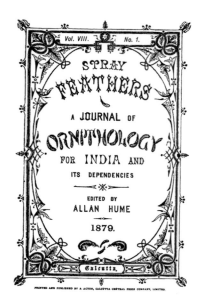

Stray Feathers

he was away from home, an employee sold the manuscript in the market for waste paper. The following year, a deeply dejected Hume presented his entire collection to the Natural History Museum in London. Earlier, in 1872, he had started the journal *Stray Feathers: A Journal of Ornithology for India and its Dependencies*. He was its editor and chief contributor, and published descriptions of his new discoveries such as the Hume's Owl, Hume's Wheatear and Hume's Whitethroat. Using his contacts and position in the civil service, Hume built up a network of well over 200 ornithologists writing in from various parts of India. Images were, of course, indispensable and apart from the ornithologists, skilled artists were pressed into service by the indefatigable Hume. The journal was published until 1899 when he discontinued it, as by then he was living in England.

A man of immense intellectual and physical energy, Allan Octavian Hume, combined a challenging career in the civil service – he had had a significant role to play in Etawah district during the uprisings of 1857 – with his interests in ornithology and theosophy, writing extensively on both. Hume took early retirement in 1882 and three years later, was one of the founders of the Indian National Congress. Even after his return to England, he remained general secretary of the Congress for several years. Hume's death in 1912 was widely mourned in the colony as he had clearly established himself as a committed friend, one who believed that the British needed to be more self-analytical about their continued role in India. Interestingly, he is less remembered for his contribution to the fledgling discipline of ornithology.

CHARACTER
IN HIGH PLACES

⤙⤚

*H*ow did a foremost plant-collector of his times deal with a tremendous fear of heights and of the cold? Frank Kingdon Ward spent a large part of his life in the mountains and his twenty-four expeditions into the wilds contributed to a transformation of the early 20th-century Western garden. Like many of his day who encountered the East, he was a racist if not an imperialist, and yet, aware of the 'we-they' divide, admired the sturdiness of the hill people. For him, plant-collecting was mere expediency – a means of garnering funds for his true ambition which was to be recognised as a geographical explorer. However, in spite of his best efforts, Kingdon Ward never quite made it to the ranks of established adventurers, explorers and mountaineers.

A reading of *In the Land of the Blue Poppies* with its graphic accounts of swinging across gorges on fragile bamboo strands and spending nights alone in crevasses with a howling wind for company, makes one wonder how Kingdon Ward dealt with his fear of heights. Robert Macfarlane (*Mountains of the Mind*) has some answers: mountains have had an irresistible attraction that came to possess people – mostly men. One mountain in particular possessed George Mallory for years and killed him in the end. Macfarlane looks at how a mountain that was 'after all, just a mass of rock and ice' took over so totally the mind and body of a man devoted to his wife and three children. At some level it was not difficult to understand, for as Macfarlane wrote, 'Everest is the greatest of all mountains of the mind … And no one has been more attracted to Everest than George Mallory'.

It was this obsessive involvement that helped in overcoming fear: to the imperial Briton it was also a sign of manliness (which, today, Macfarlane says, would be regarded as machismo) to push one's limits. In 1863, author and critic John Ruskin wrote to his father from Chamonix that if one turned away from 'a dangerous place' when it was prudent to do so, one's *character* … suffered some slight deterioration' as one became 'more lifeless, more effeminate, more liable to passion'. On the other hand, going through with the danger, one came out 'a stronger and a better man', fit for every form of work and tribulation; '*nothing but danger* produces this effect,' Ruskin wrote rather self-righteously.

As the Empire settled in, Macfarlane felt that 'Victoria's burghers became increasingly fond of risk-taking'. Mountaineering was a 'danger valve' – one that provided an outlet for the steam that built up 'through cosseted urban living'. Macfarlane added that patriotism was also an emotion aided by 'the mystical power of mountains' and the idea of the suffering yet striving mountain climber had a singular appeal to the fascist mindset; Adolf Hitler was a strong believer in dangerous climbing routes and the conquest of heights. If this might sound a bit extreme, Macfarlane quotes Leslie Stephen – author, mountaineer and father of Virginia Woolf and Vanessa Bell – who felt that 'the authentic Englishman' wandered in the wilds, amidst dangerous terrains, coming as close to 'breaking his neck as his conscience will allow'.

The camera, by then an essential prosthesis of the Raj, could hardly be ignored by the intrepid explorer and mountaineer. Such feats of conquest and valour had to be recorded and it was the work of the arch-imperialist, Samuel Bourne, that provided among the earliest photographs of the Himalaya. Bourne's talent and vision surpassed most visual recorders of India. Between 1863 and 1866, he undertook two Himalayan expeditions where he was accompanied by a retinue of at least thirty coolies. In an article written in the literary style of the times for *British Journal of Photography*, he lamented that 'but how many lovely and charming pictures are there in the secluded valleys in the ravines of these mountains that never have been, and never will be portrayed by the camera'. And as for the mighty Himalayan range, 'it is altogether too gigantic and stupendous to be brought within the limits imposed by photography'. Often enough, 'in the places where the best points presented themselves there was not standing room for my tent or even camera'.

A prodigious worker, Bourne was not one to be daunted, often taking enormous risks in photographing the rare and the beautiful. At the end of his first trek lasting ten weeks, he returned with 147 glass negatives. Bourne was not so lucky on the trek to Kashmir the following year as his hapless porters dropped a box of eighty-four glass plate negatives (12 inches × 10 inches). Although he managed to salvage a few, another twenty were affected by damp. On his second Himalayan trek, Bourne was able to photograph the Manirung Pass at an elevation of 18,600 feet. He commented triumphantly, 'I am not aware that any other photographs have ever been taken at so great an elevation as this'. Even if they had 'been less perfect than they are I should still have valued them, and they would have been interesting on this count'. Samuel Bourne issued a catalogue of 1,500 photographs in 1866 and later, numerous photographs were reproduced in several volumes, many of them by the well-known studio of which he was a partner, Bourne & Shepherd, with its branches in Calcutta, Bombay and Simla.

The scenic beauty of the Himalaya and of Kashmir made the production of albums very lucrative indeed for several photographic studios, including that of William Baker and John Burke in Murree. The image of a peak in the Pir Panjal range by William Baker in the 1860s was one of a set of four views of the range in the north-west Himalaya that separates present-day Jammu province from Kashmir Valley. More than half a century later, Frank S. Smythe, British mountaineer, author, photographer and botanist, was to take some amazing photographs in the Himalaya. In 1931, he trekked to a delightful valley full of wild flowers not far from Joshimath. This was to become the Valley of Flowers National Park. Smythe felt that the paintbrush with its daubs was no match for the camera: even though at first sight 'it seems a hopeless task to squeeze a noble mountain several thousands of feet high into the humble dimensions of a film', composition was of

A peak in the Pir Panjal range. Photograph by William Baker, 1860s

the essence. Nor was this easy as unlike the artist who can choose, the photographer was often beset with 'muddling details'. Hence, simplicity was of the essence, and though 'never in my life have I taken a photograph that completely satisfies me', he persisted, illustrating his many books, including *The Mountain Scene*, with impressive mountainscapes. He believed that it was always better to 'suggest than reveal in photography', often inevitable in mountain photography. Those impressed with the grandeur of a mighty peak might overlook the fact that 'height, size and colour when reduced to a small photograph suffer greatly in quality'. Such photographers needed to be constantly reminded of the limitations inherent in the medium; yet, the role of the photograph as an effective mnemonic device was of growing significance. Trekkers, mountaineers, imperialists or mere tourists, could hardly not value an image that extends 'the scope of memory far beyond one particular scene'.

VICEREGAL WHIMSIES

⟍⟋

When, in the 1880s, Edwin Arnold, former principal of Sanskrit (later Deccan) College at Poona (Pune), and a well-known journalist and poet, arrived in Agra by train, he was delighted with the railway station. He felt that it would be 'difficult to find a railway station anywhere which lands its passengers upon a more remarkable scene'. To the right one saw the minarets and domes of the Jumma Masjid and to the left, the 'vast red walls and bastions of Agra Fort'. Before visiting Taj Mahal, Arnold reflected back on his earlier visit made shortly after 1857; a close friend had been killed during the disturbances and he silently paid the 'private debt of recollection due to this one of many unrecorded English heroes'. After such a sombre beginning to his otherwise memorable visit, Arnold proceeded to explore the environs, recording in precise detail various aspects of the monument and its gardens.

It is possible that Arnold had a camera — or someone with him had one — and took a photograph of the Taj, adding to the growing repertoire of visual and descriptive imagery around it. At the time, the 1850s photographs taken by Dr John Murray were the most striking, while in 1783, William Hodges was the first British artist of repute to paint the Taj, over a century before, François Bernier had written about its ambience of water courses and expansive walkways. Thomas Daniell and his nephew, William, had not only painted the Taj but also produced a small book of their prints entitled *Views of the Taje Mahal at the City of Agra in Hindoostan, Taken in 1789*.

Thus, when George Nathaniel Curzon visited the Taj for the first time in 1887, he had plenty to help him reflect about 'the entrancing spectacle, the singular loveliness of it pouring in waves over my soul and flooding my inner consciousness'. Arnold's photograph provides us with a view of the Taj and its environs prior to Curzon's growing interest in the reorganisation of this classic Mughal garden. In her book on British gardens in India, *Flora's Empire*, historian Eugenia Herbert writes at some length on the controversial viceroy's intervention in the landscaping of the Taj. Interestingly, though Curzon bombarded the Archaeological Survey of India (ASI) and a whole posse of horticultural experts with views on how the redesigned gardens should look, his diktats did not seem to reflect the views of Capability Brown, the pre-eminent landscape designer of the 18th century, or even those of his own contemporary, landscape diva Gertrude Jekyll. Like much else in his 'reign', Curzon, apparently, relied a lot on his own views of what the Taj gardens should look like. He had, of course, been to India three times before he became its viceroy in 1898, visiting monuments and gardens each time. Though he observed that the Taj was in 'perfect condition', he felt that the gardens needed considerable attention – keeping in mind the need 'to restore nothing that had not already existed, and to put up nothing new'. Herbert observes that though the mausoleum itself escaped Curzon's designing eye, the gardens were another matter.

The photograph from Arnold's *India Revisited* as well as more detailed images of the Taj gardens are most useful for a historical reconstruction. In particular, one by the brilliant 19th-century botanical artist, Marianne North, shows dense foliage of trees and flowering shrubs. Curzon wanted none of that and as Herbert observes, 'set out to turn the Mughal gardens into an English park' with an orderly line of cypresses and low shrubs; the mausoleum, the pristine jewel in white marble, was to dominate and not be obscured by excessive vegetation. This was clearly a move away from the original landscape and as Herbert perceptively reminds us that for the Mughals 'the garden setting was as important a statement as the tomb itself'. She added that historically such gardens were important spaces that

THE TAJ MAHAL, AGRA.
Page 212.

'*The Taj Mahal, Agra.*'
Photograph in India Revisited *by Edwin Arnold, 1886*

often preceded the monuments. At a more formal level, important State visitors were received and entertained in them, poets recited their verses to an appreciative audience seated in comfort amidst perfumed bowers and, at times, armies were encamped in the ample lawns as well. The Mughal garden could be a focus of conviviality, of merriment if not bacchanalia, one where a verdant, somewhat overgrown expanse, nevertheless kept in mind the boundaries of geometric parterres. Thus in the 1830s, Fanny Parkes wrote appreciatively of the abundance of fruit trees, of bird song and of the rainbow colours of the flower beds.

All this was soon to go as George Nathaniel Curzon set about sanitising the Taj gardens. While respectful of the detailing basic to the structure of the parterres, 'English flowers' were banished in favour of lawns, and mahogany trees and palms, unnecessary obstructions to the vista, were pruned or removed. The viceroy had decided on how those who flocked to the Taj should view it: with little thought to historicity. Curzon mediated a new viewing for the eager tourist. The monument that had occupied

Taj Mahal and gardens. Photograph, c. 1920s

such a special place in his heart was to glow in all its ethereal beauty from the minute one entered the forty-two-acre precincts. There was to be no competition from the gardens, even if this meant felling old trees and bushes that had been chosen and planted with such care by those to whom a garden was a space almost as sacred as the tomb.

The Taj complex occupied Curzon from the very moment he arrived at Government House in Calcutta. As one of his biographers commented, 'Agra … knew the fearful joy of five Viceregal inspections in six years' (quoted in Herbert); each visit was followed by precise salvos aimed at the hapless officials of the ASI: the cypresses were too thickly planted; was it not possible to find bigger plants? Garish flowers needed to be removed; there should be more lawns ... and so on. Even as he was machinating to send Francis Younghusband to Tibet and planning on the Partition of Bengal, Curzon was continuing his interminable barrage of memos to the ASI and working on the Ancient Monuments Bill. As work on the Taj complex neared completion, J.H. Marshall, who had been appointed the ASI's director general in 1902, commented with some misplaced bravado that the Taj and its environs could 'hardly have looked more effective in the days of the Mogul Emperors than it does now'. There were others too who defended the viceroy's foray into redefining the landscape around the Taj: fruit and fragrance trees had been greatly admired – but perhaps Bernier and Tavernier had seen only young growth – and not the tangle of later years, they demurred.

Tall claims, indeed, which can be judged one way or the other with the copious visual and written material generated on Taj Mahal over several centuries. A careful study of North's paintings and the many photographs taken prior to 1900 do indeed show rich vegetation and umbrageous trees through which the monument rises. The Curzonites altered much of that, and the contemporary viewer sees the Taj through the eyes of a 19th-century Western imperialist who felt that he could better the Mughal Empire's aesthetic sensibility. He was not wrong in assuming that it is to the monument to eternal love that people throng from all corners of the world; the environs, he felt, must be kept tidily in place. Yet, one may well ask, was George Nathaniel Curzon justified in modifying for generations to come the context of that 'snow-white emanation starting from a bed of cypresses?' Or, for that matter, why, armed as it is with a rich visual history and landscape and horticultural expertise, has independent India not thought of interrogating this surprising colonial intervention and recreated the clearly legitimate vision of yet another older imperial power?

'Agra Fort. The Jasmine Tower'
Photograph by Samuel Bourne, c. 1860s

Points on a

Compass

ARTISTS & PHOTOGRAPHERS

Bourne & Shepherd

Talbot House
SIMLA

8, Chowringhee Road
CALCUTTA

11, Esplanade Road
BOMBAY

COPIES OF THIS PORTRAIT
CAN BE OBTAINED AT ANY TIME
THIS OR ANY OTHER PORTRAIT
ENLARGED TO ORDER & PAINTED
IN OIL OR WATER COLOR.

Verso of cabinet-size photograph, Bourne & Shepherd studios

LENS ON
THE GREAT GAME

⌒✕

*I*t would perhaps not be an exaggeration to say that visual artists do not usually write about their oeuvre – but when they do, the reader gets an amazing glimpse into the workings of creative minds. Not always pleasant or affable with those he worked with, the photographer, Samuel Bourne, had a facile pen that brought alive his treks in the Himalaya. He wrote a number of interesting articles in *British Journal of Photography* which not only provided details on technique but also evoked the beauty of the landscape and terrain that he had explored, often under fairly dangerous circumstances. A bank clerk from Nottingham, Bourne came out to India in 1862, by which time he had been experimenting with the camera for a while. Though it is not clear why he came to this country initially, he soon turned his seven-year sojourn into a paying business proposition. He became the major holder in a lucrative partnership in the Bourne & Shepherd chain that had studios in a number of cities.

Not as well known – perhaps also because they did not leave behind narratives of their work and travels – but no less talented were the duo, William Baker and John Burke, the earliest commercial photographers in the North-West Frontier. Omar Khan provides a fascinating account of an integral aspect of British rule – its war machine – through the work of these two men. In 1861, William Baker, a retired army sergeant, started photographing in the area between British India and what was at that time Afghanistan (present-day Pakistan); some years later, he was joined by John Burke, a 'teenage assistant apothecary from the Royal Artillery'.

However, sensitive to the requirements of the market, the Peshawur (Peshawar) studio of Baker & Burke did not concentrate only on military photographs and, although Burke was not greatly interested in the picturesque, he took many photographs of architectural monuments as well as of ethnic types – ubiquitous nautch girls, the viceroy's camp at Lahore in 1894, views of Lahore fort, spacious roads in Rawalpindi and so on. At this time, although Kashmir was outside British India, its scenic beauty attracted numerous European tourists, and the catalogues of Bourne & Shepherd and that of Baker & Burke provided more photographs of the region than of any other location. A steady demand from those who could not escape the hot, dusty plains but 'yearned for images of cool scenery even grander than what they may have remembered of Europe' ensured a substantial market – and many prizes at photographic shows.

By 1867, collaboration between the two men who had built up impressive portfolios individually was formalised, and the studio, Baker & Burke, opened first in Peshawur and soon after, a branch office was started at Murree, where Baker became one of the founding members of the Murree Municipal Committee. The town had an influential British population and within a couple of decades, Colonel Sir Francis Edward Younghusband, 'one of the most celebrated and controversial heroes of the Great Game', involved as he was in information-gathering well beyond British boundaries, was soon to become among the best-known figures of the region. He was born in Murree to army officer John Younghusand, and Clara, and his family was keenly interested in family photographs; there are fanciful portraits of his parents in 'Yarkhand Costume' and a carefully composed 1874 side view of Durdens, the Younghusbands' Murree home. The image has all the attributes of a stage set with John standing on the veranda, and Clara in a *jhampan*. Both are positioned to the viewer's left while the right of the frame is occupied by the *bhisti*, *darzi*, *doodwala* and other domestic servants. In the front is a group of women, ayahs, who tended to pupils at Clara's home school for the servants' children. Francis,

MEMORIES OF BELONGING

then twelve, was away at boarding school in England. He shared this fate of enforced separation from the family with scores of children of the Raj; a number of both men and women later recounted those days of close to abject misery in memoirs, letters and journals. The aim of the photograph was quite clear: to memorialise as well as serve as a mnemonic device for the Younghusbands and, more importantly, for the wider kin group back home. Families needed to be reminded of what colonial life implied; it was hard work in inclement climates among an alien and often recalcitrant people. If it provided an elaborate lifestyle, this was merely just compensation for many hardships and perceived deprivations. A steady source of income for photographers came from European families as well as some Indians eager to be photographed in the *carte de visite* and cabinet-size formats.

Clearly though, for John Burke, excitement lay in pictorialising war and destruction – and not in creating stage-set-like images of prominent British families. Soon, the younger man garnered an impressive portfolio by accompanying military expeditions to Afghanistan. Between 1838 and 1919, the British conducted several military campaigns in the area and the photographing of the Second Afghan War of 1878–80 – 'the defining struggle of the Great Game'– became a high point of Burke's career. By this time the partnership had come to an end. In 1873, Burke had set up offices in Murree and Rawalpindi. So as to take a range of military and official photographs, he kept shuttling between cantonments in the North-West Frontier and the Punjab. Much later, Burke opened a studio in Lahore. In 1878, he travelled with British troops as they invaded Afghanistan, taking thousands of photographs during the two-year conflict. Apart from their usefulness to the military establishment, his two major catalogues had high commercial value as well.

There is not much blood and gore shown of the Great Game but rather some very interesting compositions of groups such as 'Officers of Her Majesty's 51st Regiment on Sultan Tarra' where three Afghans have been placed at a point much higher than the British soldiers – 'a typical Burke twist on the expected composition of Victorian imagery of Europeans and natives' (Khan). Here the pecking orders of race and class are deliberately subverted. Burke repeats this twist in the image taken near the Khyber Pass

'Peshawur Valley Field Warriors Resting Against a Hillside'
Photograph by John Burke, Khyber, NWFP, 1878–79

in 1878–79, titled *'Peshawur Valley Field Warriors Resting Against Hillside'*.
Again, it is a meticulously composed shot, with the position of each of the
seventeen men carefully worked out. All except one are 'locals'. The eye
strays to the man in the second row from the top, clad in a dark tunic and
striped turban. He is seated behind a boulder and does not engage with
the camera but looks into the middle distance through his arresting light
eyes. He is Colonel Robert Wharburton, an Anglo-Afghan, the son of an
army officer and an Afghani of noble descent. The rulers obviously used his
mixed parentage to advantage, appointing him political officer in Khyber
Pass; his task was to bring to heel the Afridis, regarded by the British as
the most aggressive of all Pathan tribesmen. Wharburton was apparently
rather successful, writing of the Afridis' 'great devotion' once the barrier of
mistrust was done away with. John Burke was commissioned to take this

photograph of Wharburton with a group of men with whom he worked. Although heavily armed, the body language of most is fairly relaxed; the aim of the photograph was perhaps not to represent a fighting force ready for action, but to document the usual workspace of the British army in those inhospitable terrains.

At a time when Baker and Burke were in business, although photography within the studio was the norm, professionals had to be versatile enough to lug their paraphernalia and relevant staff to outdoor locations. The two men appeared equally at home with the camera within enclosed spaces as well as on site, whether this meant taking images of a snowbound landscape in Murree or of the detritus of battlefields. It was significant that the formal structure of a studio photograph or even a painting of a family or group was carried over to the outdoors. The directorial role of the photographer continued to be crucial, and though important clients like the Younghusbands or Robert Wharburton must have had their say, it is likely that considerable negotiation as well as mock shoots preceded the final exposures. By the early decades of the 20th century, things started changing and the studio was no longer the sole repository of the camera, nor the professional photographer the possessor of a unique skill. Photography became a part of middle-class life worldwide. Quite often the camera was a prized accoutrement in the hands of the domestic photographer charged with the responsibility of recording the life and times of an increasingly visual population. The elite may still have hired the likes of Bourne and Burke, but for most, Kodak's Brownie was a cheaper and less time-consuming option.

Lilah Wingfield at Chandni Chowk, Delhi. Photograph, 1911

TEA PARTIES AND
TONGA TALES

⟨⟩

hile the association of travel with self-discovery sounds clichéd, for those women virtually imprisoned by the moral codes of upper-class life, being able to get away from it all was indeed liberatory. For the single British woman, who either became a member of what came to be known somewhat unkindly as the 'fishing fleet', travelled to visit family, look for jobs or take up positions of governesses and so on, the East held endless promise and indeed hope. In a recent book, Anne de Courcy looks at girls and women who formed part of the fishing fleet from the 17th century onwards and concludes that courtships could range from a few days to a month or so. Interestingly, she adds, concerned over the fact that the British in India were either setting up liaisons with local women or marrying them, the East India Company actually sent out young single women 'whom they maintained in India for a year, during which time they were supposed to find a mate … if after the year they had proved too plain or too unpleasant for even the most desperate Company man, they were shipped home as "Returned Empties".'

This most derogatory term that underlined the seriously skewed gender relations among the British in India drew attention not only to the ubiquity of matrimony and the unenviable status of unmarried women but also to the purported eligibility of those in the service of the Company and later of the Raj. What it did not acknowledge was that some young and not so young women chose to travel on their own to the East and experience its promise of supposed magic and fascination. For them, the hope of potential adventure often had little to do with the relentless search for a spouse.

Particularly among women travellers and of course, residents, letter and memoir writing and, for those with artistic talent, drawing and painting were almost mandatory; in the pre-camera days, keeping time aside for memorialising or sharing became an important part of the day's agenda. It is more than likely that only a fraction of what was written survives; these writings and visual imagery provide an exclusive rendering of different and differing understandings and experiences of India. Some women lived an entire lifetime, most days more humdrum and stressful than exciting, while others came for visits that became life-changing and momentous. Undoubtedly, social background and opportunity determined what India could offer to women who either came through compulsion or through a yen to travel. For the lucky few, the choices were more glamorous and promising than it was for others.

When Lilah Wingfield saw an enticing advertisement in *The Illustrated London News* for journeys to India during the Royal Durbar of 1911, she wasted little time in making plans for a trip. It would provide the lively twenty-three-year-old of Anglo-Irish aristocratic descent a way of escape from her controlling mother. Soon, armed with watercolours and a camera, and with a companion, a chaperone and a male escort she was on the P&O liner, *Maloja*, headed for Bombay. The serendipitous acquisition of her diary by her granddaughter, Jessica Douglas-Home, led to a reconstruction of Lilah's life and although the focus was on the star-studded days at the Durbar, the intrepid Lilah travelled afar, to Bangalore (Bengaluru) and Benares (Varanasi) and then to Peshawur (Peshawar) and Rawalpindi. The North-West Frontier and the Khyber Pass had a distinct fascination for many British women; few perhaps also remembered – or had indeed heard of – the incarceration of the formidable Lady Florentia Sale, wife of General Sir Robert Sale, second in command to General Elphinstone, who headed the British military presence in Afghanistan. Sale had been sent to clear the

Khyber Pass. Photograph, c. 1900s

access to the Khyber from Kabul of Ghilzai Pashtun rebels. In the bitter winter of 1842, a seriously outnumbered British army was nowhere near achieving its task and in no position to rescue their stranded families; soon, unable to undertake the march, often on foot and through deep snow, to join her husband in Kabul, Lady Sale agreed to become a prisoner of Akbar Khan, son of the Amir, Dost Mohammed (from Singer).

To some this might have seemed like a strange if not dangerous choice to make; they, however, did know what the march to Kabul meant for women. Often, they were robbed of their possessions and left only with the clothes on their backs. Or, for example, Mrs Mainwaring had to walk through snow carrying her young child, picking her way 'over the bodies of the dead, dying and wounded'. Crossing endless streams of freezing cold water, avoiding the gunfire of the enemy and not quite knowing where one was headed were terrifying experiences. When the unfortunate woman got to the camp, there was no chance of being able to change her clothes; Lady Sale sympathetically commented that 'I know from experience that it was many days ere my wet habit became thawed and fully appreciate her discomfort'. Little surprise, then, that Lady Sale chose to become a prisoner. Known by now as the 'grenadier in petticoats' the redoubtable lady kept a detailed diary of those eight months in captivity. The dozen women and twenty-two children held as prisoners were well treated and Akbar Khan even earned some respect from Lady Sale; he allowed a celebration of her wedding anniversary by arranging a dinner with the ladies of her captor's father-in-law's family. It is another matter that the recipient of this favour wrote of the event with characteristic disdain: her hostesses were coarse-featured, their dress inelegant and 'they ate with their fingers, Afghan fashion; an accomplishment in which I am by no means *au fait*. We drank water out of a teapot'. Had she mistaken the variant of a samovar for a teapot, one wonders?

It was to the Khyber Pass, too, that Lilah was headed, although she found time to explore Peshawur beforehand, escorted by a bodyguard to protect her from 'the outlaws from the mountains'. On December 22, 1911, Lilah and her party chose to set out in a tonga with the aim of reaching Jamrud Fort at the mouth of the pass before nightfall. They took the more interesting, although perhaps less comfortable, option, though a branch of the North Western Railway covered the short distance of 10 miles between Peshawur and the fort. The mud battlements were built by the Sikhs in 1826 and witnessed a bitter Afghan-Sikh battle a few years later. The Sikhs won the war and although it looked vulnerable and unprepossessing, the fort's strategic location was to make it invaluable to the British. At the fort, Lilah and her party changed into two-horsed tongas 'in which we rattled along in fine style'. As they cantered and trotted up the steepest, most rocky paths with aplomb, Lilah was greatly impressed by the 'lean-looking little horses from Central Asia which are used in these mountain tongas'.

Determined to reach the limits of British India, Lilah and her party pressed on to the fort at Ali Musjid passing 'crowds of different tribes from the heart of Asia' tramping along. She noted a large rock at which caravan-loads of Muslim travellers disembarked to pay homage. The rock was reputed to bear the mark of a kick from the Prophet's horse when he had ridden through the area 1,300 years ago. The fort at Ali Musjid too was not much more than worn out battlements on a plateau above a hill – although it had been the scene of the first battle of the Second Afghan War of 1878. Their final destination was the last British outpost of Lundi Kotal (Landi Kotal on the Khyber Pass) that provided a panoramic view of the border of India with Afghanistan and

'Gamrood Fort'
Photograph, c. 1900s

the road to Central Asia where few Europeans dared venture. Snow peaks stretched into infinity and Lilah could not but marvel at 'such fine virile men' who guarded the frontiers. Unsettled times meant that the visiting party had to leave well before dusk and an overwhelmed Lilah wrote that 'the sun going down over the tops of the mountains at the entrance to the Pass was something I shall never forget'. In spite of some minor dalliances and a more serious one with a Captain Amir Ahmed, Lilah did not acquire a husband on her Indian trip; however, it was not long after her return that she made an appropriate choice and, as her granddaughter added 'watched from afar the fortunes of those she had encountered on her journeys through India'. She was an inspired 'empty' who came back brimming with excitement: Lilah shored up her many experiences by writing engagingly about them in her diary and filling red and gold leather albums with innumerable photographs.

Bremner, Lahore.

A BEND ON THE SIND RIVER, KASHMIR.

'A Bend on the Sind River, Kashmir.'
Photograph by Fred Bremner, c. 1880s

AN 'INFORMED' VIEW
OF KASHMIR

⤙

A residence in India often lent itself to creative expression of various kinds, even though the number who combined a job with a hobby in writing, photography or art may not have been very large. A number of colonials who are best known for their works in imaginative fiction, spirituality and homemaking, such as Rudyard Kipling, Edwin Arnold and Flora Annie Steel, also wrote the odd essay or even a book on their travels or impressions of this land that fascinated and intrigued them. Then there were those who had gained fame, if not notoriety, in other fields and yet wrote volumes on a range of completely unrelated subjects – Colonel Sir Francis Edward Younghusband being among the best known. One of the most celebrated and controversial heroes of British expansion in the north, Younghusband had single-handedly masterminded the invasion of Tibet in 1904 and is generally regarded as one of the protagonists of the Great Game between Britain and Russia. Younghusband's early explorations of Manchuria in 1886, when he was a young man in his early twenties, opened up routes unknown to the British and he returned to India across Tibet, charting inhospitable terrains. For his pioneering and hazardous trek, he was elected to the Royal Geographical Society, its youngest member, and received the society's coveted gold medal.

After the Tibet expedition, Younghusband became the British Resident in Kashmir. He wrote over thirty books on various subjects: significant treatises on realpolitik, the mystery of Mount Everest – as president of the Royal Geographical Society, Younghusband was one of George Mallory's strongest supporters – a book on South Africa and later, on religion and faith. He had strong attachments to Kashmir and the north of India as he was born in Murree, where his father was an army officer. Though he is hardly remembered as a travel writer or informed guide, in his book *Kashmir as it was*, the somewhat uncompromising imperialist-cum-spy provides an interesting, but not terribly well-organised, account of a region much favoured by the British; it also allows us to think of Younghusband, albeit grudgingly, as someone who responded with great empathy to nature and his environs – and not only as an ambitious man interested in massacring and overcoming recalcitrant 'natives'. The slim book is part potted history combined with personal reminiscences and 'artsy-crafty' tourist information on what to look for and perhaps buy. There is also an entire chapter devoted to the new invention of hydroelectric power being harnessed by a Major Alain de Lotbinière, a Canadian engineer who had been employed by the maharaja.

Younghusband's writing accompanied formulaic though attractive reproductions of paintings by Major E. Molyneux. The original book, published in 1910, with seventy plates of Molyneux's watercolours must have been a treasured possession as, by then, Younghusband was an iconic Raj figure. As British Resident in Kashmir, Younghusband had all the resources required for long equestrian treks into the hinterland, and on *shikars* in pursuit of the *barasingha*, the Kashmir stag. This involved riding through snowy mountainsides, and though often the trip was infructuous, Younghusband wrote that 'a day like this on the mountainside is felt as one of the days in which one lives'. A bit of an amateur birder, he supplies the interested reader with lists of birds to be seen in various seasons, and for the collector of wildflowers, there is plenty to look for amidst the boulders, nooks and crannies. On Srinagar, Younghusband has much to say, as for him it was clearly the most beautiful city of the East; it was the 'combination of picturesque but rickety houses, of mosques and Hindu temples, of balconied

Shikaras on Dal lake with a mosque in the background. Etching, c. 1920s

shops, of merchants' houses and the royal palaces with the broad sweeping river and the white mountain background' that made it so charming. The ceremonial arrival of the Maharaja of Kashmir from Jammu, when he entered the summer capital by boat, is described in much detail: the two flotillas – his own as Resident and that of the ruler – as well as the excited shouts of '*eep eep ra*' ('hip hip hooray', one presumes) from many hundreds of schoolboys carrying flags, and the final arrival at the palace.

Colonial town planning could not but take into consideration the requirements of racial segregation, Munshi Bagh being the European settlement. The Residency, with its well laid out gardens, was an important marker (Younghusband writes at length about his garden), as were the 'tidy little club', the parsonage, Parsi shops, the post office as well as the bungalows of the British working for the state of Kashmir. And then strolls along the Bund had to be mentioned, a high point in the city's busy social calendar. Younghusband concludes his chapter on Srinagar with notes on places of interest: Shah Hamadan Masjid, close to the river and built of wood with beautifully carved eaves, Dr Neve's mission hospital, the Dal lake, resplendent with lotuses in July and August, overlooked by the Takht-i-Suleiman with its ancient Hindu temple and, of course, the famous *baghs*. Younghusband has much to say about Mr Nichols of the Archaeological Survey, and his attempts at restoring the garden and pavilion of the Shalimar Bagh: while restoration emphasised the original formal structure of the gardens, Younghusband felt that 'to fall in with the ways of Nature may be the best method of adding to the existing beauty of the garden'. The enthusiastic author takes us to Gulmarg, where the structure of Srinagar is replicated: a smaller Residency, European homes and the famed golf course and polo grounds. Most important, away from Srinagar, the visitor could remain anonymous, avoid the whirl of social activity, and 'need not speak to a single soul unless he wants to'. He could pitch his tent in the wilderness and 'take his solitary walks in the wood' – and yet, a social life was close at hand when he tired of his own company. That possibility was perhaps rare, as the natural beauty of Gulmarg would keep the traveller fully engaged: meadows full of wild flowers, forests of spruce, blue pine, maple and the odd horse-chestnut against the backdrop of snowy peaks.

The contemporary reader may despair at the lack of structure in *Kashmir as it was*, or even tire of some rather prolix extolments of natural beauty; yet, the book is valuable not only for an account of what today's violence-ravaged Kashmir was really like less than a century ago, but also because it is among the few volumes available on towns and cities in colonial India. This book is, more than anything else, his tribute to an area that he loved, knew extremely well and in which he had a considerable influence at a time critical for British strategy in northern India. Nor does he skimp on detail or information – hardly surprising, as Francis Younghusband was, as his biographer, Patrick French feels, proficient in many things, with a facile pen as well as a spiritual side to his personality. He is purported to have had a mystical experience in Tibet, and became, in later life, extremely religious, founding the World Congress of Faiths in 1936.

ORIGIN MYTHS
AND
EARLY HISTORIES

_Origin myths of what today are well-known places are fascinating not only because of the lore associated with them, but as descriptions of 'those days' allow imaginative encounters with the past. This is particularly so as often, not much of original structures and institutions remain; fanciful reconstructions are possible through a reading of those detailed repositories of information, the District Gazetteers, memoirs, newspapers and the odd work of fiction as well as by looking at paintings, prints and photographs. Indian hill stations, many of which are being systematically destroyed by the ravages of real estate prospectors and developers, are particularly suited to this kind of mental exercise. As these were so coveted by the rulers eager to find reprieve in a better climate, a few first-hand accounts of the times are available – and some by Indians are fraught with instances of racial discrimination and accepted hierarchies.

When, in the 1930s, Congress politician Murli Manohar Joshi's stepsister, Tara Pande, and her doctor husband moved to Naini Tal (Nainital) with its charming lake, she found it 'a beautiful and lively town, quite different from the old-fashioned, hide-bound Almora of my childhood'. However, 'we Indians were not allowed to walk on the Mall Road – that was reserved for the whites. There was another path that ran a few feet below, reserved for the natives.' At the same time, Shakuntala, niece of the leading nationalist political figure Govind Ballabh Pant remembered going to a school run by 'a Christian lady whom we simply knew as Miss Sahib'; more than formal teaching, they 'were sent to Miss Sahib to learn the rudiments and to smarten up a bit'. The Pants were syncretists – Western etiquette for girls could coexist harmoniously with a deep commitment to an independent India (from Gokhale).

When Edward James (Jim) Corbett was born on July 25, 1875, at Naini Tal, he was the thirteenth child of his enterprising mother, Mary Jane. A 'Mutiny' widow with four young children, Mary Jane married Christopher William Corbett in 1859. She had been among the hundreds of refugees to flee from Agra in 1858, making the journey to the safe environs of Mussooree (Mussoorie) by an assortment of man-borne 'vehicles'. Not long after their marriage, Christopher was to become postmaster of Naini Tal and the journey from one hill station to the next was not easy. Once more, Mary Jane and the children travelled in a *doolie* not unlike a *palki*, borne on the shoulders of four strong men. The final ascent was in a *dandi*. During the 200-mile-long journey through rough paths and jungle tracks, the chances of coming upon the odd tiger, if not a gang of dacoits, was very real.

The couple had nine children of whom Jim was the last but one. His mother was the redoubtable matriarch of a family that had invested heavily financially and emotionally in Naini Tal and its environs. Not long after settling in the town, Christopher Corbett bought land in Kaladhungi and built a house in close proximity to the *terai* jungles in the foothills. The present 30-odd miles of motorable road between Kaladhungi and Naini Tal are surely not what Corbett and his friends would have taken; to them the obvious choice was the *pakdandi* – a short cut through 'more or less dense forest' interspersed with bits of cultivated areas. Records trace the discovery of Naini Tal to 1841, when a Mr Barron who had been looking for a salubrious spot chanced upon the area with its natural lake. There are two theories regarding the lake's origin: one, that it was excavated by glacial

Sailing on Naini lake. Photograph, c. 1930s

action and, second, that it was caused by a landslip. Barron was 'enthusiastic over the beauty of the scenery, the crystal clearness of the water, and the plentiful animal life'. By 1843, he had built Pilgrim Lodge, which was later to become one of the cottages of the club.

A 1927 account in a collection of essays on Naini Tal by L.C.L. Griffin, assistant commissioner, provides us with an interesting aside on the politics of hill stations: in a publication called *The Hills*, a writer with the nom de plume of Bagman accused Barron of gross exaggeration: the lake was stagnant, unhealthy and the roads were dangerous to a pedestrian. Barron and friends, it went on, were giving Naini Tal publicity only to press their own advantage. Not to be put down, Barron wrote that he knew of the 'despicable' author who went shooting 'crawling on all-fours and wore a pair of green spectacles'. Given that not too many persons were likely to have this interesting taste in glasses, Bagman's identity was sure to remain no secret. His attack was apparently fuelled by an apprehension that the new hill station might soon rival the older ones of Mussooree and Simla. Perhaps commercial interests underlay his proprietorial attitude.

In 1857–58, the town was buzzing with refugees from Agra, Moradabad and Bareilly; it was not long before the 'natives' got restive, only to be dealt with severely by the commissioner, Major Ramsay, who immediately declared martial law. There were rumours of some hangings as well. Things settled down, and Griffin noted wryly that, judging by the letters exchanged between residents and 'friendly' Indians in the plains, 'the chief material need was for beer'. Ramsay was well in control of the situation, resisting attempts to send women and children to Mussooree: the hill people, he argued, had no sympathy with 'the rebels,' and relocating populations 'would disturb the present quiet, and make a panic throughout the district,' he wrote.

Not one to lose control or have others question his authority, he was to later become Major General Sir Henry Ramsay, and as he 'ruled' the region for over twenty-eight years, he was known as the King of Kumaon. While at the helm, Ramsay was able to make Naini Tal the summer capital of the United Provinces. This was in 1862, and it soon became a favoured spot for Europeans and some affluent Indians, and also a suitable venue for educational institutions, the best known being Sherwood College.

By this time, demand for properties to buy or to rent had gone up exponentially; as Corbett's biographer, Martin Booth, points out, sensing an opportunity, the astute Mary Jane Corbett soon set herself up as 'Naini Tal's first estate agent.' She not only sold cottages that she had got constructed on choice plots, but also rented them out for the season or more. Things changed somewhat after the landslip of 1880 that killed over a hundred people. Thirty-three inches of rain fell between September 16 and 19, and as there were deep crevasses left from the clearing of sites for new developments, in no time 'the whole hillside was one mass of semi-fluid matter, and required little to set it in motion'. The Victoria Hotel was completely buried by a section of the hill that 'had descended with enormous velocity and violence'. Of the 151 dead, forty-three were Europeans or Eurasians, and there was considerable destruction of property, including the temple dedicated to Naina Devi. The force of the landslide carried the temple bell to a spot across the lake, where a new shrine was erected the following year. Mary Jane was indeed relieved that her family was intact; however, as the prices of houses plummeted, her business was badly affected. After her husband's death in the following year, Mary Jane

Jim Corbett with a fish caught in Naini lake
Photograph, c. 1930s

built Gurney House on the Ayarpata Hill, not far from the lake. The couple had bought the piece of land as investment a decade before and though it was not in a fashionable part of town, it was on stable land.

While the landslide shook the morale of residents and those interested in investing in Naini Tal, this was not for long. It was soon back in people's social calendars, reflected in Rudyard Kipling's 'The Tents of Kedar', an episode in his *The Story of the Gadsbys*. The town's chatterati are at an elaborate sit-down dinner. Soon, 'after conversation has risen to proper pitch,' Mrs Herriott,

The Corbett home in Kaladhungi, now a museum. Photograph, c. 1930s

one of the guests, castigates her reluctant paramour, Capt. G, for neglecting her. Reluctantly, he has to tell her of his other interest. Sensing her distress, the person seated to her left comments sympathetically, 'Very close tonight, isn't it? You find it too much for you?' 'Oh, no, not in the least,' she replies quickly, though adding 'But they really ought to have punkahs, even in your cool Naini Tal, oughtn't they?' A hundred years on, fans have indeed made their appearance in Indian hill stations, the result of climate change and overcrowding rather than of a much-more-amusing Kiplingesque dramatic sequence. If they chanced to come by today, while they would perhaps recognise the odd old bungalow, Tara Pande and Mary Jane would surely quail at the sight of Naini Tal's scarred and eroded topography, jam-packed with ill-planned and unsightly shops, eateries, hotels and dwellings.

MEMORIES OF BELONGING

MOSQUITO NETS
IN A
MANGO ORCHARD

~~✦~~

*A*fter retirement from the Indian Civil Service (ICS), Herbert Charles Fanshawe wrote *Delhi – Past and Present*, a useful guidebook on the city for visitors and residents alike. Apart from being suitably embellished with stories of valour and of torture around 1857, it provides a potted history of the various Delhis, as well as interesting information from the census of 1901 and other government sources. He writes that out of Delhi's population of 2,08,000, over 50 per cent were Hindus and around 40 per cent were Muslims. The city, Fanshawe felt confident, would soon grow to be 'one of the greatest trade centres in India' as well as a substantial manufacturing hub, primarily because it was served by five different railway systems. The municipal committee 'has always been distinguished for its enlightenment', spending generously on waterworks and drainage. On the other hand, Chandni Chauk (*sic*), Fanshawe lamented, was 'sadly spoilt by the very modern frontages of many of the shops and houses'. He wrote appreciatively of Maiden's Hotel, which was excellently managed and clearly the best place to live in, situated as it was within the civil station, or Civil Lines as it was known.

No. 17. THE MAIDEN HOTEL, DELHI (INDIA).

'The Maiden Hotel, Delhi (India).'
Postcard by H.A. Mirza & Sons, 1905

Fanshawe's book predated the pomp and panoply of the coronation *durbars* of 1903 and 1911, and the shift of the capital of British India from Calcutta to Delhi. According to Rudrangshu Mukherjee, in his lengthy letter to the Secretary of State for India, Lord Crewe, Viceroy Hardinge, made an important political statement regarding why the shift was a judicious one: local self-government would flourish away from the workings of a provincial government. In any case, Calcutta was somewhat inhospitable after the Partition of Bengal in 1905 and the 'peculiar political situation' that followed. Besides, while among the masses the city was 'revered as the seat of the former Empire', Mukherjee adds that in the minds of Lytton and Curzon, choreographers of the *durbars* of 1877 and 1903, 'the notion of imperial splendour had come to be associated with Delhi'.

Even before Edwin Lutyens, Herbert Baker and the many hundreds of officials, planners, architects, engineers and so on arrived in this somewhat arid plain, Delhi had started attracting a floating population of migrants. Besides, it was also home to a number already well settled in the walled city, many of whom had proved their loyalty to the British after 1857. In time, Civil Lines became attractive to well-placed Indians such as the large extended family of St. Stephen's College-educated Rai Bahadur Raj Narain; two of his granddaughters, Sheila Dhar and Madhur Jaffrey, wrote delightful memoirs of their charmed lives. In *'Here's Someone I'd Like You to Meet'*, Sheila, an accomplished Hindustani classical singer, writes of the extended family where her married aunts returned to their father's home with their children as the schools were so much better in Delhi. At any given time, there were close to sixty persons who sat down to meals. Her perspicacious barrister-grandfather, Raj Narain had located his large establishment in Civil Lines in a large orchard, bought from a reward given to an ancestor by the British 'presumably for services rendered'.

Over time, family partitions resulted in twenty-four bungalows in the orchard, each with its own lawn; those relatives who still lived within the walled city 'were awed by the new Anglicized life style that was the ideal of each of these units'. Envy and admiration were the response to the breakfast of eggs, toast and jam rather than *parathas* and *bhujia*; even the women had learnt to eat with teaspoons. Only the men were entitled to forks and side plates in addition to spoons of various sizes. Scotch and soda replaced *keora sharbat* in the long summer evenings where the men relaxed on deep verandas after a game of tennis. Expectedly, such changes were hard for the women who were married into this family of British loyalists. Sheila Dhar's grandfather accepted the necessary Westernisation of his family and engaged an Englishwoman as tutor for his wife; apart from learning some stock phrases, the lady soon had her blouses adorned with ruffs and collars. She wore these with her well-starched cotton voile saris. That her puja room remained an integral part of her life apparently irked the Rai Bahadur, who 'never lost an opportunity to needle my grandmother about the hocus pocus she engaged in'. However, writes Sheila, this was possibly his official stance; he was quite relieved that his wife kept tradition alive in a fast-changing milieu.

Her younger cousin, Madhur Jaffrey (actor and food writer), titled her memoirs equally evocatively, *Climbing the Mango Trees*, and there she described a Delhi full of childhood joys, summer holidays in the hills and

'The Kutub Minar'
Photograph in India Revisited by Edwin Arnold, 1886

picnics in the monument-studded wilderness round the city melding imperceptively with the newly emerging present. Family picnics that never involved less than thirty persons were invariably a detailed exercise in planning and organisation. To begin with, all had to be packed into a Dodge and a Ford in an orderly manner; this also included pots, pans, pre-cooked delicacies and *durees* that had to be 'coaxed' into the boots of the cars. Invariably, the destination was out and beyond Lutyens' New Delhi, passing through Kashmiri Gate, St. James' Church and Red Fort on the way. Expectedly, Qutub Minar was the destination, and in the 1940s, to get to it one had to pass by fields of *sarso* and *bajra*. There were no restrictions against climbing the minaret and on a clear day, 'we children could proprietorially survey all of the Delhis below us'.

Picnics were reserved for spring and before the onset of deep winter; in summer there was the other north Indian experience of sleeping out in the open. These were pre-air cooler and air conditioner days when one would eye ceiling fans churning hot air with disgust and flee to the perfumed gardens outside. The extensive lawns were lined with twenty or more beds, each with its own mosquito net. Although Madhur and her cousins were up with the first rays of the sun, there was something primal about staring at the galaxy, looking out for a shooting star and trying not to hear the eerie 'hukka hua' of a jackal in the distance. Clearly there was no fear of thieves – or maybe there was safety in numbers.

Two days after her fourteenth birthday, Madhur was taken by her father to India Gate. This was August 15, 1947 and, after battling through crowds, the pair stood on Kingsway (later renamed Rajpath) to watch Jawaharlal Nehru and Louis Mountbatten ride by in an open horse carriage. As the Union Jack came down and the Indian tricolour was raised 'we screamed our lungs out. Thousands of caps were flung skyward. I felt giddy'. And then came the carnage and violence. The men in the family had earlier only handled guns when they went on *shikar*; now it was imperative to take them out on organised patrols. One night, the mob got frighteningly close and 'we barricaded ourselves indoors, fearing for our men still patrolling the streets'. All were safe but things were not so good in the walled city. A cousin went out to the shops and did not return for days. And when he did, 'he had lost his mind. Was he beaten, raped, tortured? He never spoke coherently after that'.

Gradually, as the Nehruvian era took over, the focus shifted to New Delhi with its imposing avenues, impossible roundabouts, distinctive building styles and the impersonality of a growing capital city. For Madhur, the newly established All India Radio, located in an interesting structure that combined a central domed rotunda with two wings, provided the opportunity for a foray into this part of the city; together with her cousins, she was often called upon to do radio plays. The authorities were assured of a posse of children, 'all of whom could be counted on to read fluently' and 'with expression'. Legacies of the Raj have had a healthy life span: diction, hybrid cuisines, picnics and Western education being significant 'spheres of influence'. And family cultures such as those of Rai Bahadur Raj Narain's clan were porous enough to blend in and absorb what was necessary to get along in the melting pot of a fast-changing metropolis.

A BISHOP IN
BENARES

⤙⤚

*T*he marketing of India as a travel destination through word images and photographs that create a world of fantasy and yearning has a respectably long lineage. The history of travel writing can be traced back to the early accounts of those who survived hard treks across the Himalaya or braved the seas to arrive at the enchanted land of spices. From the 18th century onwards, the British in India were soon to record what they saw both through word and visual images. Those in the military, administration, law, the clergy and, of course, itinerant tourists (several of whom were women), wrote accounts of varying quality, and these were often accompanied by illustrations.

Perhaps one of the most detailed 19th-century accounts is that of Reginald Heber, bishop of Calcutta. If one is able to stomach (if not studiously ignore) his pejorative accounts of the average 'native', Heber's descriptions of the countryside are worth reading for their informative nuggets. These were the years before the Grand Trunk Road and most of his journeys were on horseback and by carriage and boats of various kinds. Not unexpectedly, he wrote approvingly of 'Rhadacant Deb … whose carriage, silver sticks, and attendants were altogether the smartest I have yet seen in India'. He was of course referring to Radha Kanta Deb who wanted Lord Hastings

'A suttee – preparing for the immolation of a Hindoo widow'
Lithograph, drawn and engraved by Capt. Grindlay, c.1820s

thanked particularly for his 'protection and encouragement' of sati. Though his Christian soul recoiled from the 'heathen' practice, Heber could not but be impressed by Deb's pomp and splendour. Sati greatly tantalised the colonial imagination and the highly stylised engraving by Captain Robert Melville Grindlay (now better known as the founder of Grindlays Bank) must surely have had many takers.

Though smaller in scale, the ghats represented here shared much with the grander one of Benares (Varanasi). Despite the discordant assemblage of buildings, elaborate drapes and folds of clothing, the overall sense of urgency and of course the sati herself with outstretched arms no doubt exercised many back home. The institution of sati was regarded as macabre and barbaric – yet it had a strange fascination for those whose cultural and religious practices were clearly very different.

Heber's *Narrative of a Journey through the Upper Provinces of India from Calcutta to Bombay, 1824-1825* in two volumes is a detailed rendering of the time spent in touring and inspecting his vast see all the way from Calcutta to the Deccan. Heber's widow, Amelia, adds in the Preface that the diary-like narrative, with entries arranged date wise, was mainly recast from letters to her; she adds modestly 'a fact which she hopes will be borne in mind, should some consider that he has dwelt less upon the professional objects of his journey than might be anticipated'.

In August 1824, Heber visited Ghazeepoor (Ghazipur) and it is significant that he chooses not to mention the poppy fields or the Ghazeepoor Carcanna – the Sudder Opium Factory – sombre in its evocation in Amitav Ghosh's *Sea of Poppies*. Instead, he writes, 'Ghazeepoor is celebrated throughout India for the wholesomeness of its air and the beauty and extent of its rose-gardens' that occupied several hundred acres in the area. The blooms were cultivated for distillation into rose water and attar and, as the bishop goes on to talk about the 'English warehouse' where pure attar was available, like the cultivation of poppies for opium, clearly this was also an economic activity of the Company. One could hardly expect the venerable bishop to mention the seamier and more oppressive side of British commercial activity; the by-product of fragrant roses was one thing, but that of poppies was quite another proposition.

What Bishop Heber does mention in some detail, however, is the fact that 'suttees are more abundant here than even in the neighbourhood of Calcutta, but chiefly confined to the lower ranks'. Again, one is reminded of Ghosh's description of the powerful Kalua's rescue of Deeti from husband Hukam Singh's funeral pyre where '[R]acing to the ground, Kalua placed the platform against the fire, scrambled to the top and snatched Deeti from the flames'. Earlier, in superbly crafted sentences that release the tension of the moment, Amitav Ghosh describes how the platform had been used as a projectile to disperse a crowd of relatives and voyeurs alike. Though Heber was not witness to any such heroics, he was nevertheless greatly distressed by 'how little a female death is cared for' and resolved to have a 'conversation with such of my friends as have influence'. It is not known whether he ever met Lord Bentinck but certainly the Sati Regulation XVII of 1829 came about within a few years. Its main architect was of course Rammohan Roy – but perhaps the governor-general had conferred with the bishop as well?

In September of that year, Heber visited Benares, staying on its outskirts with friends as 'Europeans did not live in town nor were the streets wide enough for a carriage'. He spent a number of days wandering through the streets and ghats, marvelling at the 'lofty' houses, some of them even five or six storeys high – 'a sight which I now for the first time saw in India'. Revered as the 'Sirdar Padre' of the 'Sahib log', he visited the 'Hindoostanee place of worship, a small but neat chapel' and 'to the natives gave the communion, with the words in their own language'. While on visits into the city he found many 'bulls and beggars', the bishop was deeply impressed by the 'evident hum of business which was going on in the midst of all this wretchedness and fanaticism': shawls from the north, diamonds from the south and fine muslin from Dacca (Dhaka) – as well as 'those European accompanying luxuries and elegancies which are daily becoming more popular in India'.

Heber found time for engaged sightseeing and he climbed the ancient observatory, visited temples and the 'Vidyalaya or Hindoo College'. And most importantly, he observed how Benares functioned administratively: he felt that it was the best governed Indian town, as the inhabitants chose 'a sort of national guard, the chuprassies' who were merely approved of by the magistrates. While they were only about 500 in number, as the guards were elected and paid by 'respectable householders', they obviously had 'an interest in being civil, well-behaved, and attentive'.

Bishop Heber goes on to report a 'dhurna' – manifestation of the citizenry's opposition to the imposition of a very unpopular house-tax. Though not a witness, he had obviously been told of the incident in some detail. Land tax was justified, 'but the houses were their own' and though the house-owners represented, the government in Calcutta remained unmoved. The decision then was to sit in the open in '"dhurna" or mourning' or to remain motionless without food 'till the person against whom it is employed agrees to the request'. All of 3,000 persons (we can presume that they were mainly men) 'deserted their houses, shut up their shops, suspended the labour of their farms, forbore to light fires, dress victuals, many of them even to eat, and sate [sic] down with folded arms and drooping heads, like so many sheep, on the plain which surrounds Benares'. A perplexed local

Intricately carved jharokhas *and doorways in Benares' brass bazaar*
Photograph, c. 1920s

government decided to reason with a few of the 'ringleaders' – but to no avail. The neighbouring cantonment was empowered by a 'strong body of Europeans from Dinapoor and Ghazeepoor' – and of course it does not require much skill to decode Heber's euphemistic language and guess who these men were. Though there was no confrontation, the power of attrition set in soon and numbers dwindled. But not before a delegation from ten to twenty thousand started their march to Calcutta, through hills and jungles. In a few days, most melted away and the much whittled-down number was 'ashamed to proceed'.

Heber approvingly noted that the government, impressed by the determination and success of the protesters, decided to repeal the 'obnoxious tax'. And so ended the saga of one of the earliest peaceful *dharnas* of colonial India, recorded in meticulous detail by the diligent Reginald Heber.

AT THE HEART
OF BEAUTY

⌒⤫

Not all early travel writing or memoirs of India were eulogies. The country's heat, squalor, filth, 'half-naked fakirs' and so on were the usual suspects described in fulsome detail – and often, the healing touch of colonialism was extolled in even greater detail. Eliza Ruhamah Scidmore, an American travel writer and photographer and the first woman board member of *National Geographic* magazine, came to India in the winter of 1902 and wrote *Winter India*, a fairly dyspeptic and racist account of the country, redeemed by some rather fine photographs. She starts off by stating, 'It can hardly be said with literalness that one enjoys India. I had not expected to enjoy it, and it proved itself, despite its colour and picturesqueness, quite as melancholy and depressing a country as I thought it would be.' However, many of its problems were overcome 'with miracles accomplished by alien rule.' Eliza was a great admirer of Curzon, who gave 'Anglo-India daily shock and sensation', and of her fellow countrywoman, the beautiful Mary Curzon, for whom there was no rival in 'her unfailing tact and sweet gentleness.'

Christmas week in Calcutta meant extra tents for guests in the extensive grounds of Government House and soon the Empire revolved 'within the white viceregal palace.' The great event of the racing week was the

'Calcutta. Government House Throne Room'
Postcard by D. Marcopolo and Co., 1915

Viceroy's Cup, 'when all sporting India has its eye on the Maidan, remotest cantonments as heavily interested as the cheering crowds at the Oval.' A few days after Christmas, the viceroy and his wife 'hold a drawing-room' – obviously an 'in' word for an evening party – where 'the knee is bent to viceroyalty, and one train and bouquet give way to the long procession of trains and bouquets.'

Eliza found life in expatriate Calcutta similar to that in London – the difference marked by 'the innumerable turbaned and bare-footed servants, the pankha [fan], and the use of Hindustani words.' Of course, the sun shone gloriously and the *The Times* was eagerly awaited for 'the real news of the world'. The Calcutta papers provided interesting diversions such as advertisements on cinder-picking and ash-sifting rights for sale, and '20 Rhinoceroses Wanted, Rupees 2000 each', while Allahabad's *The Pioneer* came later in the day with snippets of local opinion voiced by colonials. December in Calcutta meant 'summer heat in noon', when European women wore 'the white gowns of the tropics at that high social hour.'

It was time to move on to Darjeeling in 'the most absurd little narrow-gage [sic] cars, with only canvas curtains as protection from the changes in mountain weather.' Eliza clearly had no idea about the expertise required in creating this marvel of the Darjeeling Himalayan Railway (DHR), the world-famous Darjeeling 'toy train' that covered 7 miles and ascended 1,000 feet an hour. This two feet gauge railway that continues to this day was specially designed in Manchester with funds raised entirely in India. Much of the credit lay with a Mr Prestage, agent of the East Bengal Railways, who not only conceived of the project but also saw to it that the line, with its many loops, was completed in record time.

Once in Darjeeling, Eliza's caustic pen gave way to eulogy as she sat waiting at Tiger Hill 'in the lee of a boulder, wrapped in rugs and razais [duvets], our veins freezing in that thin icy, mountain-top air.' She could not help but comment that 'even the tourist's perpetual-motion tongue was silenced as the colour pageant proceeded.' When Kanchenjunga appeared 'with half of its height snow-covered, so transcended all one's imaginings that it did not seem the vision could be reality.' Mount Everest, however,

The famous double loop of the Darjeeling Himalayan Railway at Tindharia
Postcard by D. Marcopolo and Co., 1910

'sulked in a tent of clouds westward.' Writing some years later in *The Heart of Nature, Or The Quest for Natural Beauty*, another arch imperialist – but one with a far less acidic eye when describing India's natural beauty – Sir Francis Younghusband was overawed with the mountainscapes around Darjeeling. The town, he felt, 'ought to be set apart as a sacred place of pilgrimage for all the world' situated as it was amidst forests of oaks, laurels, rhododendrons at whose base grew violets, geraniums and lobelias; hillsides covered with ferns and orchids looked on to the snowy ranges, making it a place where one could contemplate 'Nature's Beauty in its most splendid aspects.' Younghusband was less lucky than Eliza – or perhaps more realistic – as he alerted the traveller to the hours and days to be invested in the hopes of a satisfactory Kanchenjunga-viewing. However, 'one minute's sight of the mountain would satisfy him … for a moment the current of his being comes to a standstill.' As is true of many splendiferous sights, nothing one has ever heard or read about them ever measures up to what one sees, and for the person who has sighted the great mountain 'henceforth and forever, his whole life is lifted to a higher plane.' Though at times the mist of the region hid much, Younghusband felt that this veil revealed more than it concealed – the true spiritual nature of the mountains. Relying on some rudimentary knowledge of geography, Younghusband felt that the blue of the region was quite different from the blue of Greece, Italy and the Alps. It appeared to have more body, 'a *fuller* colour, a bluer blue, a purpler purple than the atmosphere of these other countries.' Such depth of colour provided a more pleasing warmth from the sun. He marvelled at nature's palate as the greens of the foreground gave way to washes of pink, violet and purple while the snowy ranges varied from 'decided rose-pink in the early morning and evening to, perhaps, faintest blue or violet in the full day.' These were set against the backdrop of a sky dyed an intense blue.

Younghusband cited the experience of the noted Russian painter of battles, Vasily Vereshchagin, who had visited the region in the 1880s. He organised himself to paint the third highest mountain in the world and even as his wife kept handing him brushes and paints, he was unable to place colour on his canvas. He is reputed to have said, 'not now, not now; it is all too splendid.' Vereshchagin could never paint the Kanchenjunga though

Kanchenjunga at dusk with Darjeeling in the foreground. Photograph, c. 1930s

he had no problem in painting *The Apotheosis of War,* a spine-chilling visual documentary of destruction – human skulls arranged in a pyramid against a stark landscape. Younghusband must also have approved of Vereshchagin's dedication of the painting 'to all conquerors, past, present and to come.' In 1903–04, on orders from Viceroy Curzon, Younghusband led an expedition into Tibet, ostensibly to solve a minor border dispute; what resulted was a horrendous massacre of Tibetans, including several monks. On the way back, Younghusband apparently had a mystical experience, which led him to believe that all humans were divine – and to regret his actions in Tibet. Hardly surprising then that for a man committed to adventure and conquest in the name of Empire, he saw in the Kanchenjunga a glow of 'the pure flame of undaunted aspiration.' Even if his days of violent action were over when he visited Darjeeling, he could not help but note that 'between ourselves and the mountain is the kinship of common effort towards high ends.' Not unexpectedly, Francis Younghusband's last years were spent tending the World Congress of Faiths that he had founded in 1936.

'Robinia Suberosa'
Hand-coloured illustration in Flora Indica *by William Roxburgh, 1832*

William Carey sent the seeds of this plant from the district of Dinajpur to the Royal Botanic Garden at Calcutta.

BOTANY
AS ENTERPRISE

*P*lant-collecting that became a part of colonial exploration was rarely an innocent, Sunday afternoon exercise: it was exacting, highly competitive and at times, physically dangerous. The work of the early 20th-century plant collector is best exemplified in the writings of Frank Kingdon Ward, an intrepid collector whose books document his several years in the Himalaya. A shy Englishman, Ward was terrified of heights and hated the cold. Clearly a person of conflicting emotions, he was able to overcome his primeval fears and spend long months in expeditions focussed not on climbing high mountains or remote passes but in collecting minute botanical specimens. In the process, of course, he undertook many perilous journeys and became a premier plant collector of his times. While Joseph Hooker first took Sikkimese rhododendrons to Britain, Ward inherited the task of introducing more cultivars to eager gardeners back home. His descriptions of the plant collector provide fascinating insights into a less known aspect of the imperial project − the collection and naturalisation of rare species. Plant-hunting, Ward wrote *In the Land of the Blue Poppies*, is not like big-game hunting; it is a job undertaken to earn bread and butter through a love for flowers. The plant hunter, he wrote 'does not make up a cheery party of congenial spirits, and go off for three months on full pay'.

Rather he goes alone, for several months 'without seeing or speaking to another white man. And sometimes it hurts'.

By the time Kingdon Ward was ready to retire from the field, pioneering collectors and naturalists had been succeeded by a tribe of commercial plant hunters. However, as he noted, 'it is indeed certain not only that we have as yet only skirmished on the fringes of botanical Asia' and although there was fierce competition to find a 'new' specimen, he felt that 'the true collector derives just as much joy from finding a plant which is new to him whether it has already been "discovered" or not'. And in any case, there was plenty of scope to keep taking back 'old friends' who were dying out because of the 'ill-treatment of our presumptuous climate'.

Kingdon Ward was an entrant in a by then established field of collectors – horticulturist-administrators, painters and housewives – but he made botany an enterprise that combined professionalism with a keen commercial edge. As the discovery of plants increased with European imperialism so did the understanding of the Other in plant taxonomy. 'Exotics' were those that had come from abroad, often from the tropics, and 'natives', the local residents. The many garden plants of the Western hemisphere that are treated with such familiarity today had origins as varied as China for the peony and camellia, the Himalaya for the rhododendron, while the Damask rose came from the gardens of Damascus and the best-known bromeliad, the pineapple, from Christopher Columbus' second trip to the New World; he found it being cultivated by the Carib Indians in the West Indies. As the number of plants available for horticulture, medicinal use and garden adornment increased, the importance of classifying as well as studying them scientifically was acknowledged. An earmarked space seemed appropriate and, by the 17th century, the idea of the botanic or botanical garden came into being.

While today botanical gardens may have become tourist destinations with well-demarcated zones for plants, herbs and trees, their essential purpose remains that of scientific experimentation and discovery, sometimes with the marketable angle in mind. When the amateur botanist, Captain Robert Kyd of the East India Company, proposed the setting up of such a garden in Calcutta, he initiated a new chain of thought. There was a

'The Eden Gardens, Calcutta'
Photograph in India Revisited *by Edwin Arnold, 1886*

growing recognition of the need to not only classify local plants but also to 'improve' them as well as create an ambience for commercial products such as cotton and tea. Thus, in 1787, the botanical gardens were established on well over 200 acres. With more than 12,000 trees and 1,400 species, the Acharya Jagadish Chandra Bose Indian Botanic Garden, as it is known today, is the oldest and most extensive garden of its kind in Southeast Asia. During Victoria's reign it was known as the Royal Botanic Garden.

Among the several names associated with early Indian botany, the father and son duo of William and Joseph Hooker, Nathaniel Wallich and Johan Konig are significant. The latter introduced Linnaean taxonomy to India, greatly helping the classificatory process. While William Hooker never came to India, he was an indefatigable letter-writer and his detailed correspondence with Wallich is an impressive reflection on botany. A number of others involved with Indian botany had in one way or another been associated with the East India Company's Garden or the 'Company Bagan', later known as the Royal Botanic Garden; the new garden in Calcutta included a teak plantation that supplied valuable timber to the ship-building industry and new crop varieties that Kyd hoped would be able to avert 'the greatest of all calamities, that desolation [caused by] Famine and Subsequent Pestilence'. Kyd was succeeded by William Roxburgh, who, together with the Baptist missionary, William Carey, another keen amateur horticulturist, set up the Agricultural and Horticultural Society of India. The profit-making impetus was further hastened under Roxburgh. The new superintendent realised that botany could help in the identification of plants to be used as dyes and for sacking while the usefulness of different trees in construction could be experimented with. Thus plant taxonomy continued apace with research on the economic viability of plants and trees and in no time, plant collectors throughout the country started sending specimens for identification to the garden. In addition, the superintendent of the botanical gardens had another task – teaching botany in the city's medical college.

After Emily Eden came to visit her brother, Governor-General George Auckland in Calcutta, the Auckland Circus Gardens was renamed Eden Gardens in honour of the two sisters, Emily and Fanny – and long before it entered the annals of cricketing lore, it was a pleasure garden. Emily found that while some Europeans were genuinely interested in botany and horticulture, for the majority, the Royal Botanic Garden too was the venue for a convenient and pleasurable outing away from the heat and noise of the metropolis. Several decades later, girls from the Bethune School and the Hindu Mahila Vidyalaya were taken in curtained phaetons for a day's outing to the well laid out gardens. By this time too, among the Indian upper and middle classes, the gardens at Calcutta became a favoured destination for carriage rides on many a winter day or summer evening. Apart from many new interesting flora on view, the prime attraction at the Royal Botanic Garden was the 250-year-old banyan tree, which at present has over 3,000 aerial roots and spreads over an area of four acres.

As expected, the tree with its myriad aerial roots held promise for the umpteen photo studios in the city and in no time, photographers from Bourne & Shepherd studio found it an interesting locale; there is an early 20th-century photograph of Lady Curzon seated before the many roots of this amazing tree. Such images, however, had a limited and somewhat exclusive viewership as they were part of expensive books and albums. Keeping in mind the wider market for views of the Raj, Bourne & Shepherd

Avenue of Palms, Botanical Gardens, Calcutta.

'Avenue of Palms, Botanical Gardens, Calcutta.'
Postcard by Rapahel Tuck & Sons based on a photograph by
Bourne & Shepherd studios, 1904

soon decided to sell images to the well-known London-based postcard manufacturers, Raphael Tuck & Sons. By the end of the 19th century, such postcards were readily available and at a fraction of the price of a photograph. The 1904 postcard of the avenue of palms at the Royal Botanic Garden has the trademark figure, a *mali*, positioned beneath an imposing specimen: Bourne & Shepherd was well known for its use of humans to give a sense of space, size and atmosphere. The structure of this pre-1907 postcard was quite different from its successor as above the image there was a blank space for messages and the undivided reverse was for the address. While botanical knowledge may have been limited to a few, the role of the visual through the photograph, the postcard and the detailed botanical illustration, helped bring a little known aspect of the Raj at work into the domestic space.

'A Cockatoo on a Branch'
Watercolour on paper, c. 1850–1890

OF PAINTERS
AND
PRIESTS

$\sim\!\!\sim$

*I*n the 19th century, visual representations of the country and of Indian life through various art forms, including the increasingly popular camera, acquired a unique purchase. Some, such as those inspired by artists of the Company School, the work of the Daniells, William Hodges, Balthazar Solvyns and so on spilt over from the 18th century; later, the photography of men like Samuel Bourne, Linnaeus Tripe and Raja Deen Dayal were encouraged by the British while other visual specialists were self-consciously 'home-grown', such as the Kalighat *patua* or *chitrakar* artists of Calcutta. A history over the last 200 years of the evolution of the Kalighat *patachitras*, a series of vibrant images, and the individual image or *pat* could lead to an inspired (some might say quirky) understanding of aspects of the Bengali psyche. It is at times an extremely suggestive visual genre, weaving narratives with a certain unerring painterly ease. In fact art historian Partha Mitter has attributed the appearance of 'caricature as a systematic weapon of social criticism' to this school of indigenous visual satire.

Morning worshippers at Kalighat Temple, Calcutta
Photograph, c. 1930s

It was after the construction of the new Kalighat temple in 1809 with its traditional *athchala* design that the serious migration of *patuas*, painters on handmade paper scrolls or *patachitras*, to the region began. The art historian, Pratapaditya Pal (1990), feels that though the art form took off after the first decade of the century, *patuas* and *kumors* must have been living in and round the area for much longer. They were essential for pilgrims and the devout, providing imagery and votive vessels for worship, both at the site and within homes. Pal adds that though religious iconography was the *raison d'être* of this genre of painting, the *patuas* used an 'imaginative power' rarely seen in other artistic traditions of the country. He focuses on two early scrolls representing Hanuman and Jatayu from the *Ramayana* where both are dealt with sympathetically: rather than stress the failure of the aged bird to prevent Ravana from abducting Sita, Jatayu is portrayed as a 'hero of cosmic proportions'. A huge Hanuman clasps his outsize heart within which sit Rama and Sita. He looks into the middle distance, eyebrows arched, eyes thoughtful. Pal wonders whether this imagery was borrowed from the 'Sacred Heart' representations of Christ. If not, one would add, it meant that the artist had a fine – if somewhat fanciful – understanding of anatomy.

Whether it is a courtesan decking herself or Bhima killing Kichika in the *Mahabharata*, it is the eyes that become the point of focus in this school of skilful, popular art. For instance, in the much reproduced image of a not quite rotund Ganesha, the elephant-headed god has amazingly 'human eyes'; they beckon the viewer, encouraging a range of emotions – a feature of many Kalighat paintings of the 19th century. In time, the art form appealed to certain sections of the rulers; among them, interestingly, was the staff of missionary schools, where it is possible that the explicit, multi-hued – the particularly bawdy were surely excluded – images may have been used by them as effective counterpoints in the 'civilising' role of puritanical Christianity. Travellers and tourists in search of the unusual souvenir also honed in on these as did serious aficionados, sometimes endowing their collections to institutions. Thus, today, the Victoria Memorial Hall (VMH), Calcutta, has a small though significant holding, while London's Victoria and Albert (V&A) Museum has the largest collection, owning over 600 large water colours, hand-coloured lithographs and line drawings as well as almost 300 postcard-size images.

Among the better known collectors whose acquisitions are with the Museum were Rudyard Kipling's father, John Lockwood Kipling, a teacher and a sculptor based in Bombay and Lahore, and former ICS officer, W.G. Archer, who became keeper of the Indian section of the V&A in 1949. In collaboration with established Santiniketan-based painter Mukul Dey (a serious collector of Indian art) Archer was able to enhance the museum's collection. Significantly, as Suhasini Sinha, the curator of the joint VMH and V&A's 2010–2012 touring exhibition of the paintings points out in the accompanying catalogue, *Kalighat Paintings* edited by her and C. Panda, then

'Bangali Babu'
Watercolour on paper with tin detail, c. 1870–1890

curator of VMH, Dey was one of the first artists to pay serious attention to this genre; in 1932, he lamented that with the arrival of the printing press and of lithography, '[T]hese pictures have now entirely vanished. The artist craftsmen are nearly all dead and their children have taken up other business.' Museums and private art collections, he added, have become 'their last asylum'.

At a time when the *patuas* started painting, they had only a selection of natural pigments and dyes to work with: red from the crushed leaf of the teak or *segun*, blue from the brilliant-hued though common *aparajita* flower, yellow from the turmeric or *haldi* root and so on. These were used in vibrant images of women in bright clothes, birds, fish and flowers. In their informative essay entitled 'Material and techniques of Kalighat paintings', Michael J. Wheeler and Lucia Burgio point out that detailed examination of a couple of images showed preliminary tracings in pencil that were then filled in with colour. Often, production of several images in a day was the outcome of these ateliers, with the various tasks being shared out among a number of artists under the overall supervision of the master artist. In time, particularly between the 1840s–60s, a few adopted lithography to produce the lines of the main images.

Proximity to the Kalighat temple meant that religious themes dominated the initial years with many renderings of the terrifying Kali, Shiva on his favourite bull, Nandi, Durga as *Mahishasuramardini*, Vishnu sleeping on the serpent, Ananta, Narasimha and an entire range of paintings dealing with the life of the much-loved Krishna. Most of these would have appealed to a devout audience, the several different poses catering to varied sensibilities. Of greater interest for a non-religious, discerning audience are those categorised in the catalogue as 'Social Commentaries, Proverbs and Animals'. A charming one of the *shial raja* (the jackal king of the jungle) brings alive smiling jackals while that of the 'Bangali babu' lampoons the life of the foppish Calcutta dandy with his Western-style closed shoes and 'Prince Albert' hairstyle; in other *pats*, he plays the sitar or indulges two yapping lapdogs and so on. Women are represented as goddesses, wives or courtesans and it was not unusual to depict them in positions of dominance – though of course, the reality may have been quite different. A brightly painted *pat* of a buxom woman, with the sari arranged in a manner that outlines her ample breasts, shows her leading her lover, depicted as a sheep, on a string. In another, she holds a peacock. While both women drape their saris in the conventional style, only the former wears a blouse. Some images more than others indicate sensitivity to changing dress codes as, by this time, the 1870s, the sari-blouse had been introduced.

The ambiguous position of women in a changing society is best exemplified in over a dozen evocative individual *pats* that narrativised what came to be known as the Tarakeshwar Affair. An unchaste wife – Elokeshi – is beheaded by her husband Nabin when he gets to know of her affair with the Mahant (high priest) of Taraknath temple near Calcutta. Both Nabin and the Mahant are put on trial and *patuas* competed with an excited media and a popular theatre to represent the entire affair. In the final image, the Mahant waters plants in the prison garden, overseen by a British official who towers over him. This larger-than-life representation of the white man symbolises the latter's power in a skewed racial context, enabling the viewer to internalise visually the ruler-subject relationship.

Patuas used artistic license to lampoon, entertain, inform and indeed, on occasion, remind a subject people of their place in an unequal relationship. More than many other visual practitioners, the Kalighat artists were able to cock a snook at Bengali society; on occasion, at a time of considerable flux, they even drew satirical attention to the complexities as well as ambiguities of the colonial experience.

BOMBAY
FOR ALL PEOPLE

*C*ommenting on the Bombay of the 19th century, sociologist Meera Kosambi drew attention to the composition of its rapidly growing population: a 'large spectrum of racial, religious and linguistic diversity, arranged within a broadly hierarchical and non-competitive pyramid'. At its apex were the Europeans followed by the mercantile communities, mainly Parsis and Gujaratis, while Marathi-speakers – by far the dominant group – were the non-commercial literary elite as well as the backbone of the clerical and labouring categories. Kosambi adds that until the mid-19th century, urban Bombay consisted of the Fort or the 'European Town' and the Native Town that spread out north of the Esplanade. While the mercantile communities resided close to the Fort, the Maharashtrian population lived in the more sparsely populated peripheral rural areas. Not surprisingly then, well into the middle of the century, urban Bombay comprised the Fort and the Native Town, and it was not until 1864 when the first census of the island was taken that the semi-rural localities known as individual towns and villages became encapsulated into Bombay city.

Kosambi draws attention to the fact that the first detailed description of the fast-growing region was written not in English but in Marathi by Govind Narayan Madgavkar. Apart from a brief history, the author regales the reader with details of many sites – the docks, cotton mills, educational institutions and hospitals – and also provides a sneak peek at prominent personalities. He wrote of the 'marvellous things' that lured many to migrate to this region of 'tall mansions, huge buildings, lovely bungalows, and parks and gardens'. Contemporary accounts by foreign visitors, too, could not but notice the increasingly varied character of the area and, after a second visit in the 1880s, English poet and journalist, Edwin Arnold, wrote of the 'tide of seething Asiatic humanity [that] ebbs and flows up and down Bhendi bazaar'; he also noted that the streets of Bombay were crowded with 'Arabs from Muscat, Persians from the Gulf, Afghans from the Northern frontier, black shaggy Biluchis, negroes of Zanzibar, islanders from the Maldives and Laccadives, Malagashes, Malays, and Chinese' who 'throng and jostle with Parsees in their sloping hats, with Jews, Lascars, fishermen, Rajpoots, Fakirs, Europeans, Sepoys and Sahibs'. Clearly, Bombay by the end of the 19th century was a polyglot, multiracial melting pot, heavily dependent on the coexistence of newer modes of transportation such as the train and the ocean liner with the ancient dhows of the Arabian Sea.

The 'magnificent new railway station' (Arnold) caught the immediate attention of many. Calling it a structure built as a grand 'culmination of the canonization of steam', Bill Aitken reminds us that at the time, the Victoria Terminus (today's Chhatrapati Shivaji Terminus or CST) was the largest 19th-century structure; its grandeur apparently led a dyspeptic vicereine to comment that it was 'too good for the natives'. Built in the Bori Bunder area, the station was completed in 1887 to commemorate the Golden Jubilee of Queen Victoria. Combining various architectural styles with a certain degree of over-the-top panache, the architect, F.W. Stevens, thought nothing of creating what was to be a purely functional building on the lines of an artefact; nor apparently did the government of India demur at footing the bill. A flight of imaginative fancy could lead to questions of whether generations of bustling travellers ever had – or have – the time or the inclination to admire the elaborate dome or notice the embellishments and nooks so carefully positioned. They would however, surely comment on the role of the station in bringing India closer.

When, in the 1880s, Yamuna, the heroine of Hari Narayan Apte's social

Victoria Terminus. Photograph, c. 1890s

novel, *Pan Lakshyat Kon Gheto!* first saw Victoria Terminus, 'the very sight of that huge station frightened [her]'. Stevens's creation had thoroughly intimidated the young woman – 'the reaction aroused by the sight of this enormous station can be imagined only by one who has undergone the experience,' she commented. Although she was bewildered by what she had seen from the train window – mills and chimneys 'touching the sky'– there was much more to come. The buildings were already seven storeys high as against the more modest three storeys of Poona (Pune) to which Yamuna was used and, finally, there was the miracle of the tramway. While the multi-storeyed building no doubt brought a new kind of lifestyle where the front door could shut the world out, it was quite a while before the bungalow was to disappear.

Bombay was an exciting and interesting place to be in, one where middle- and upper-class women found space for greater gender equality. Apte's Yamuna might have been daunted by the size and grandeur of Victoria Terminus but she was soon to revel in the free atmosphere of a city where mixed social gatherings were not unknown. For these of course, appropriate attire was de rigueur, and progressive sections among the Parsi and the Muslim communities had done much towards developing ways of draping the sari, and the new blouse. It was after all in the Bombay of these days that Jnanadanandini Tagore observed Parsi women's draping of the *gara* and the use of the *sudreh* and jacket. As the wife of ICS officer Satyendranath Tagore, a suitably attired Jnanadanandini went to soirées, parties and meetings with her husband as well as to zenana gatherings meant for women only. She was soon writing back enthusiastic letters to members of her family in Calcutta about the sari blouse. In a society where most women still did not wear stitched garments, the introduction of the blouse was liberatory indeed.

By the time Atiya Fyzee, from the well-known Tyabji clan, came to live in Bombay, it was more than acceptable for the girls and women in the family to be educated and to host zenana gatherings. Atiya and her sisters were sent to study at the Zenana Bible Medical Mission (today's Queen Mary's High School for Girls) located conveniently near their home in Mazagaon in south Bombay. As the area had been possibly established by the Portuguese, it had a substantial Catholic population, providing a natural catchment area for the school. While the family was not unduly worried about the chance of proselytisation, the girls were given additional lessons in Urdu, Persian and the Quran and might even have had an English governess to teach them the piano and singing. Even more important was their role in the late 1880s in the setting up of the Tyabji ladies' club, Aqd-e Surayya, Necklace of Pleiades. This was no casual *adda* group for women in the family, rather it had a constitution, minutes, a rule book. Eschewing strict norms of purdah, the club invited both 'gentleman and ladies' to meetings, provided the appropriate office-bearer had granted permission. Members were keen learners and were soon to be greatly excited with and involved in the series of talks given by their cousin Ameena on her travels in Europe. This was in 1894, and a little more than a decade later, Atiya was to board the P&O liner from the bustling Bombay docks. She was on her way to London to train to be a teacher (Lambert-Hurley and Sharma).

Illness interrupted Atiya's ambition and although she did not finish her course, she had learnt and imbibed enough to join the unique Tyabji custom

Studio portrait of
Lady Bachoobai Nowroji Vakil
c. 1890s

of writing journals and autobiographies. The tradition was apparently started by Camruddin, older brother of Badruddin Tyabji, an early president of the Indian National Congress, and soon various branches of the family in Bombay and elsewhere were also keeping detailed notebooks in each home. Known as *Akhbar ki Kitab*, five such volumes of these accounts written between 1860 and 1878 are part of the Fyzee collection that is housed in Bombay University. A rich repository indeed of life in this evolving metropolis. For a dominant leitmotif that links present-day Mumbai to old Bombay continues to be its potpourri-like character, memorialised in celebrated buildings, life stories, fiction and, of course, Bollywood extravaganzas.

View of Rajabai Clock Tower taken from the gardens of Bombay University
Photograph, c. 1920s

A TALE OF
TWO BUILDINGS

*I*n 1857, even as distrust, tension and violence spread through north India, the British established universities in the three presidencies. The University of Bombay owed much to the munificence of two Indians, Cowasjee Jehangir Readymoney and Premchand Roychand for its splendid buildings designed by the renowned British architect, Sir George Gilbert Scott. Interestingly, both philanthropists – a Parsi and a Jain – came from the Surat region of present-day Gujarat. Apparently, Readymoney's offer of one lakh rupees galvanised the government into thinking about buildings for the university. However, it required acerbic letters from the benefactor to get the bureaucracy moving: at the end of four years with no plans – let alone a building – in sight, he wrote a letter of complaint to the governor, Sir Seymour Vesey Fitzgerald, saying that 'Government machinery is so unwieldy that a force of elephants could not move it unless Your Excellency takes personal interest'. Earlier, he had written to the university administration asking for his money to be returned 'with usual interest of 5 per cent'.

As expected, the generous Readymoney did not take back the grant, possibly after he got to know that part of the problem lay in the logistics involved in designs making their way from Scott's studio to Bombay. It could not have been easy for cumbersome plans to move to and fro between London and Bombay; fine-tuning in keeping with local conditions needed to be passed by Scott, well known in England for designing public buildings, churches and parsonages as well as restoration work including that of the cathedrals at Coventry and Ely. As over 800 buildings were either designed or altered by him between the 1830s and 1877, he must have been a very busy man and no doubt punctilious about standards. Nor is it known whether he knew the local architects in charge of implementing his plans in Bombay. Not unexpectedly, matters reached a flashpoint more than once, as both Scott and those in charge in Bombay felt severely tested by the unusual situation of thousands of miles separating the architect and his brainchild.

Bombay's University Hall finally opened in 1874 with a floor area of 6,000 square feet, an apse, galleries and even an organ loft; seating was to be provided for 400 examination candidates and acoustic principles had to be in line with the overall climate of Bombay where, in the monsoons, an overwhelming sea could send high winds whizzing through the building. In recognition of Readymoney's largesse, his coat of arms was emblazoned on either side of the hall. Over time, the pure Gothic building with its curved ogee windows, buttressed balconies, elaborate arcades and numerous niches for statues became, according to Jan Morris in *Stones of Empire*, one of the Empire's 'most admired, abused and unmistakable structures'.

When it was finally completed in 1878, the Rajabai Clock Tower of the university was the tallest building in the city; standing at 280 feet, it towered over the bustling city, a grand structure with an impressive carriage porch in the front built to accommodate the many fine horse-drawn vehicles that came by. Statue niches housed large figures carved out of Porbunder stone, abiding examples of the Orientalist view of different costumes and, indeed, races. At an even higher level, the various communities who had made Bombay their home were represented in another set of statues. The clock tower was built from a generous endowment of two lakh rupees made by Premchand Roychand, the son of a rich businessman from Surat. A founding member of the Bombay Stock Exchange, Roychand memorialised his mother by naming the tower after her.

'University Gardens and Clock Tower, Bombay.'
Postcard by Clifton & Co., 1905

He obviously had a commitment to learning as, from 1866 onwards, many a brilliant student at the University of Calcutta who has received the prestigious Premchand Roychand scholarship would have had occasion to remember the man whose foresight led him to endow higher education in a city quite different from Bombay. Like the University Hall, the tower too was designed by Scott, its Gothic orientation unmistakeable. In addition, it had fine, stained-glass windows and an interesting spiral staircase. It was, however, the peals of its bells that marked out its uniqueness; striking a range of tunes, including, of course, 'Rule Britannia' and 'God Save the Queen' in the days of the Raj, this was indeed a new experience for the growing number of Bombayites.

By the time these two buildings came to dominate the Bombay skyline, education, both Western and indigenous had become important

'Bombay. Back Bay from Malabar Hill.'
Postcard by Raphael Tuck & Sons, 1905

foci of interest – and indeed investment – in the growing city. Fifty years earlier, Mountstuart Elphinstone, governor of the Bombay Presidency, the Rev. John Wilson and Jagannath Shankarsheth had done much to increase educational facilities. Elphinstone had not only concentrated on Marathi, but on English as well, and soon Elphinstone College was established. It also provided the opportunity for indigenous philanthropic initiatives and a leading citizen of Bombay, Sir Cowasji Jehangir, helped fund construction of its building. At more basic levels also, education was expanding, and a number of schools, both government-funded as well as elite institutions were set up. Earlier in 1845, Grant Medical College had been established, its name honouring Sir Robert Grant, a governor of Bombay committed to setting up such an institution. The idea of commemorating Grant was that of Shankarsheth, and Sir Jamshetjee Jeejeebhoy donated a thousand rupees towards its establishment. A law college as well as one for fine arts followed and each of these institutions was housed in well-thought-out buildings, combining various architectural styles with a certain self-confidence – if not self-conscious ease.

Domestic architecture too underwent many changes. Although the city was soon to become one of high-rises, there were still considerable variations in living spaces, the focus being on air circulation – often at the cost of privacy. The writings of R. Bentley of the East India Company give a good idea of the bungalow, as yet with a thatched roof 'and looking, for all the world, like a comfortable English cow-house'. The author was duly impressed with the fact that each member of the family occupied an entire suite consisting of a bedroom, dressing room and bathroom; most of them opening up onto the indispensable veranda. The European elite, he wrote, lived in these as well as in mansions 'with facades adorned with spacious porticos supported on pillars of sufficient width to admit two carriages'. We are introduced to a 'withdrawing-room' above the porch, something like a private boudoir, which, in turn, supported a 'light verandah-like roof'. 'Going to one's room' was hardly a private affair and involved shutting numerous doors and windows, if not partition walls constructed with venetian blinds.

That such a style of life was not limited to the rulers is clear from the later writings of Edwin Arnold. He described the mansions of the indigenous elite, characterised by stately porches, broad staircases, 'pillared halls' often with intricate marble work that were no doubt the homes of the emerging Parsi and Gujarati business leaders. He found Bombay 'a handsome city seated on two bays, of which one is richly diversified by islands, rising green and picturesque, from the quiet water, and the other has for its background the crescent of the Esplanade and the verdant bungalow-dotted heights of Malabar Hill'. Although he was a bit overwhelmed by the 'really splendid edifices' he could not but comment on the grandeur of the public buildings that were 'for the most part … a happy inspiration, which blends the Gothic and the Indian schools of architecture'. Stylistic purists and architectural cognoscenti may have had differences of opinion with Arnold and indeed with those intent on building a new Bombay. Such views are unlikely to have affected many committed to the development of a commercial hub that combined fine living with an interest in architecture. By the beginning of the 20th century, the seafront saw considerable changes with the opening of the Taj Mahal hotel in 1903 and a few years later, the

'Gateway of India, showing Taj Mahal Hotel, Bombay.'
Postcard by Clifton & Co., 1905

Gateway of India to commemorate the visit of King George V and Queen Mary in 1911.

Opulence in building styles was often a focus of the peripatetic European as well as the affluent 19th-century Bombayite. It may have been prescience, or merely the instinct to outdo ones' neighbour, that led to an interest in real estate. Whether it was the Rajabai Tower, Crawford Market or a stately home, architecture, design and building practices occupied and exercised significant members of 19th-century Bombay's ever-growing population. And there is nothing to say that things are any different today.

THE ARTFUL POSE

⤙⤚

*T*he 19th-century photographic studio brought about what art historian Partha Mitter has called 'great transformations of visual culture that broke away from earlier pictorial conventions, not least Mughal pictorial conventions'. Emergent pictorial traditions, he argues, were linked to the modernising process of India to which 'Victorian illusionist painting', processes of mechanical reproduction and finally, the camera, contributed. Yet that traces of the Mughal imprint remained integral to early photography is clear in the compositions of Indian photographers, whether in Calcutta, Madras or Bombay.

By 1840, photographic studios had started in Bombay, and according to social anthropologist Christopher Pinney who has so deftly brought into focus the photograph's wider social role, in the same year, *Bombay Times* was commenting on the daguerreotype. There was soon early institutional interest in photography: in 1855, John Harkness, the principal of Elphinstone College felt that students who had 'a taste for this useful art' could benefit from exposure to a photographer and his equipment (quoted in Allana). A number of persons applied for the post, including Narayan Daji, a Bombay-based medical doctor cum photographer. Though the department of photography did not last long, by 1857, Daji was soon regarded as one of the first known commercial Indian photographer. His series of what

Studio portrait of Raja Deen Dayal, c. 1890s

became known as ethnographic photographs predated the massive eight-volume *The People of India* project that showcased 'the various divisions of the Asian family'. The project was initiated by the first viceroy, Charles Canning in 1858, and though it involved a few Indians, interestingly, Daji was not among them.

By the last decades of the 19th century, the Bombay photographic arena, so to speak, became a significant venue for a display of talents that emphasised realism as well as the artistic uses of the medium. True representation seemed to have been the dominant philosophy of the early photographers; after all, they were displacing portrait painters and

Verso of cabinet card photograph
Shapoor N. Bhedwar studio, c. 1890s

visualisers. In 1889, Sorabji Jehangir, the chief magistrate of Baroda, put together *Representative Men Of India* – 'A collection of memoirs, with portraits, of Indian princes, nobles, statesmen, philanthropists, officials, and eminent citizens'. The volume of portraits – most were those of the Bombay gentry, including Dadabhai Naoroji – was dedicated to the Empress of India. The photographs were attributed to Vincent Brooke Day and Son, London, and George Birdwood, who wrote the Introduction, said these would enable English newspaper readers to put faces to the names that they read about or had heard of. A perceptive recognition of the growing role of the camera.

By this time, apart from Bourne & Shepherd and Raja Deen Dayal's studios, Bombay saw considerable investment as well as involvement in photography by Indians. Studios such as those of S. Hormusji, Shapoor N. Bhedwar, Bombay Photo Company and EOS Photographic Company were increasingly popular. In no time, Shapoor Bhedwar became a much sought after photographer. At the time when he worked, the interface between art and the new medium was still being negotiated; Bhedwar was able to combine fine aspects of both. A resident of Bombay's fashionable Cumballa Hill, Bhedwar went to London to study photography and was the only Indian to exhibit several images at the annual exhibition of the Photographic Society of Great Britain in 1891. In an interesting discussion of the photographer's work, Rahaab Allana has pointed out that Bhedwar emboldened a tradition in which studios were publicised as art ateliers; props of statuary, elaborate painted backdrops and a range of period costumes and appropriate accoutrement helped establish this status. Allana bases his analysis on an unusual Bhedwar album entitled *Art Studies* that has thirty-one highly stylised photographs; the patron of this fascinating volume was Sohrab Palamkote, a poet in Gujarati and a connoisseur of art. Allana feels that it might be one of 'the first Indo-European theatrical stylizations in photography'. Very carefully crafted, the posed, if not fanciful, portraits are followed by 'a staged performance piece in photographic form'.

Such representations were helped by Bhedwar's training in pictorialism where lyricism, ambience and suitable props transformed photography into an art form, creating images rather than merely recording them. In his 'The Renunciation Series', Bhedwar tells the story of Raj, a yogi, who 'captures the imagination' and fills the 'vapid empty lives' of a 'house of very attractive and idle women'. The series could have been based on an actual performance at a well-known theatre hall such as the Elphinstone or Ripon. Even if this was the case, each frame is so carefully composed that clearly there was a deep synergy between the actor or actors and the photographer, each acutely aware of the other's role in this complex rendering of a life of fantasy. In the final image, both men and women follow the yogi, giving up their material world. The photographs in this series are not only a visual treat but they also stimulate a certain curiosity about the 19th-century

'The World Renounced'
Photograph by Shapoor N. Bhedwar, c. 1890s

Bombay stage represented here; many of the actors in this series are clearly women – an interesting divergence in a profession where, as in the vibrant Parsi theatre, all parts were usually played by men. It is more than possible that as this particular play had Indians as well as European actors, presenting women on stage would not have been an issue.

In no time, Bhedwar's studio became one among many started by enterprising Indians. In his exploration of the 'studio districts' of Bombay/ Mumbai, Allana found that there was a congruence between these and the growth of the indigenous middle class. Several were located in the Fort area or on Kalbadevi Road. As with cabinet-size prints, elaborate versos were very popular; these became free advertising space for studios allowing for considerable artistic licence. Plump cherubs, winsome damsels, intertwined foliage and the odd monument were usual fare — with, of course, pride of place given to the studio's USP: an 1880s–1890s verso from Bourne & Shepherd assured those interested that not only would copies be made available 'any time', but also that these could be 'enlarged to order and painted in oil or water color'. A few decades later, it was in this vibrant commercial atmosphere that Narayan Vinayak Virkar set up his studio on Girgaum Road. Like many others in the field, Virkar's coffers were filled by 'society' photography; however, as the historian of Bombay, Sharada Dwivedi, had pointed out, his heart lay in the nationalist cause and he soon became among the first chroniclers of important personalities, Congress sessions and, indeed, the aftermath of Jallianwala Bagh.

This meant that Virkar had to travel long distances to Lucknow, Calcutta, Delhi, Amristar and Agra carrying heavy equipment. His focus, however, remained Bombay and it was unusual to have an early 20th-century political event in the city without making space for Virkar, his staff and necessary paraphernalia. Commitment to the cause of nationalism was the *raison d'être* for his photographic endeavours; Virkar's on-site work, action shots as well as portraiture of major actors in the freedom movement had moved the Indian discourse around photography a bit further afield. The pictorialist phase was soon to die out, and though realism continued to dominate, its defining lines were necessarily 'fuzzed' by the appearance of documentary photography and the photojournalist. Studios had to now compete with open spaces and their staff with fast-paced mobile units, and with incipient but eager paparazzi.

THE STORY OF
A HILL STATION

～～

*I*n 1822, Colonel Walter Sinclair Delamain, an early explorer in the region around present-day Matheran, wrote that about 20 miles (driving distance of 54 kilometres today) from Bombay harbour, he found 'very rich scenery' and 'in every direction, noble mountains'. However, a true discovery of Matheran had to wait till a couple of decades later. In 1850, Hugh Poyntz Malet of the ICS, who was the collector at Thana (Thane), happened to camp under the spur of the hill that was later to become Matheran. His early peregrinations in the region convinced him that its clean air and water made it an ideal spot for a sanatorium. In no time, early guide-books quoted both Britons and Indians on the salubrious environment of hill stations – and Matheran got special mention in some. Soon, it became a holiday retreat for Malet and a group of friends memorialised themselves in this picturesque spot that overlooked the Sahayadris: Louisa Point was named after the wife of Revenue Commissioner E.G. Fawcett; Alexander Point after a guest; and the founder of this little sylvan haven is to this day remembered in Malet Spring, a natural water source near the post office. Most English villages have the Anglican church at their centre; so too, writes Dane Kennedy, was the case with Indian hill stations and in Matheran – St. Paul's, at one of the highest points on the hill, was consecrated between 1858–60.

At the beginning of the 20th century, an ardent Matheranite, Mrs A.K. Oliver, wrote its history suitably enhanced with photographs and pithy descriptions. She informed the reader that by 1853, applications were being invited by those who wanted to lease building sites on the same terms as for the estates at Mahabaleshwar and soon over seventy applications were received; while most were by Britons – including Lord Elphinstone, then governor of Bombay – there was a fair sprinkling of Parsis, prominent among them being Sir Jamshetjee Jeejeebhoy. A year later, railway access to the railhead at Neral made life easier for those visitors and residents who had earlier crossed the harbour by a private yacht or 'bunder boat'(coastal boat) to Panvel; from there it was a 12-mile ride to Chowk, the start of the ascent. The author provided some extremely insightful comments on the decline of the area after the Share Mania of 1864–65 – speculation following the growing European demand for Indian cotton during the American Civil War (1861) – leading to 'a period of commercial failures'. A general depression of trade meant that 'for a space of nearly twenty years scarcely another house was added to the list'. The plague of 1899 changed things somewhat and Matheran became popular once more; land prices went up and a plot of five acres 'was disposed of for Rs 2,300'. In any event, by this time, as private investors were more significant than the government, a primary charm of Matheran was the absence of officialdom.

By now the town had a sanatorium and, although 2,500 feet above sea level was not much of an elevation, its main attraction was 'the luxuriance of its forests', and proximity to the sea, only some miles away, ensured a gentle breeze. The local school up to standard IV was supported by the government's 'Hill Fund' and expectedly, most students were boys, although 'a few girls may be sometimes included'. The monthly fee varied from 2 to 5 annas. While postal services had come to India in the 1840s, the local post office was only open from October to June where foreign mail letters could be posted till 6:30 on Saturday mornings. Perhaps of most interest to readers today was the Karsondas Mulji Library started by Damodar Gordhandass in a building that cost Rs 5,000. The superintendent, usually a

Name of Bungalow.	No. of Plot.	Owner.	Rent.		Remarks.
			Cold Season.	Hot Season.	
			Rs.	Rs.	
1 Castle Hill ... ...⎫ 2 Boscobel ... ...⎭	1	Jamsetjee N. Tata ...	...	...	Not to be let.
3 Paradise Lodge	2	Major M. B. Colah ...	400	800	To let.
4 The Byke	3	P. A. Hormusjee ...	400	800	,, ,,
5 Wallace's Bungalow ...	4	Messrs. Wallace & Co.	...	...	Reserved for Members of the Firm.
6 Cutch Castle (KOLLAH HOUSE)	5	Moorajee J. Narronji ...	...	...	
7 Mangaldas Lodge(FOUNTAIN LODGE)	6	Premchund Roychund...	600	1,200	To let.
8 Byramjee House ...	7	Rustomjee B.Jeejeebhoy	500	1,000	Sometimes let.
9 Gulestan	8	B. Dinshaw Petit ...	...	...	Not to let.
10 International Hotel (Pinto's)	9	....	...	...	Parsee Hotel.
11 The Hermitage and ST. JOHN'S COTTAGE	10	The Trustees of All Saints Sisters			Reserved for the Sisters.
12 Redlands No. 1. (HARRISON'S BUNGALOW)	11	⎧ Cowasjee Dinshaw Adenwalla	300	500	⎧Reserved for owner's use.
13 Redlands No. 2		⎩	...	...	⎩To let.
14 Tour Petit (WALKER'S COTTAGE)	13 A.	Mrs. Awabai Framjee Petit	...	...	

List of Houses in Matheran.

221

'List of houses in Matheran.'
in Mrs A.K. Oliver's The Hill Station of Matheran, 1905

surgeon, bureaucrat or an army officer, was the de facto 'ruler' of Matheran: he ran the library, even though it had a board of Indian trustees; was 'ex-officio Forest officer; ex officio Assistant to the Collector of Kolaba, and a Magistrate invested with such powers as may be accorded by Government to the individual officer'. He too, was available in the hill station only between October and June. After that, heavy monsoon rains made it inaccessible, and indeed unpleasant. Oliver comments that for over fifty years, the hill station managed with 'an apology for a dispensary', more than adequate proof of the 'healthfulness of Matheran'. In 1902, it was Parsi munificence that led to the establishment of the Byramjee Jeejeebhoy Hospital, set up for 'the benefit of the poor of Matheran'. In spite of such benevolent participation by Indians in the growth of the town, the British had some unique ways of maintaining racial segregation: Kennedy points out that when fires ravaged Matheran in 1865 and then in 1893, the rulers quickly used the opportunity to move the bazaar – a 'native' stronghold – out of the centre and finally, to the edge of the plateau.

Matheran was not an 'official' hill station and hence most of its revenues came from its residents, many of whom owned houses if not estates. These were often vulnerable during inclement weather and devastating storms. Oliver's book – much more than an useful addendum to the relevant district gazetteer – provides a graphic first-person account of electric storms that wreaked havoc on homes. She recalled a historic one in May 1886 in some detail. Roofs of corrugated sheeting covered with thatch became instant tinderboxes that ignited as a bolt of lightning entered like 'a globular ball of fire' rushing through rooms, setting furniture on fire, killing a servant and traumatising a chained dog. Lightning came down from the treetops to be met by tongues of fire that leapt from the ground – and strangest of all, there was a deathly silence: 'beyond a curious, swishing, hissing sound which accompanied each flash, no explosion followed'. The storm put paid to the season as visitors left in shoals – only to be back next year.

Matheran's dominant physical features are its hilltop, with rocky headlands known as points. Walking and exploring were favourite activities, and Oliver cited a most useful – if not somewhat ominous – guide provided by a Mr Maclaren, executive engineer, to various walks, their hazards and local names. Excursions should be with companions – 'or at least a coolie' as the path 'skirts dangerously near the edge of cliff [sic]'. An accident might result in a person lying undiscovered for hours; with nightfall, 'he would either have to seek refuge in a tree, till daylight showed him his bearings, or he might spend hours wandering in helpless confusion amongst a labyrinth of paths'; a moonless night would compound his distress. Not to be too discouraging, Maclaren provided a list of paths with amusing names to be followed to villages below; hence, from Porcupine Point, one needed to go down Wag Wady path and the Lak-Laky path would take one from Alexander Point to a nearby village. Even more interesting are the *tonjon* bearers' Hobson-Jobsonesque coinage of place name equivalents put together by a contributor to 'Matheran Jottings': as the bearers could hardly remember the English names of likely destinations, they had come up with their own versions: Panorama Point became Pandurang Point while Porcupine Point was Palki Point and most houses were named after their owners. After all, what else could Elphinstone Lodge be known as but 'Governor *cha bangla*'?

The real change in the life of the hill station came with the introduction of the 20-kilometre long Matheran Light Railway that links the hill station to Neral, midway on the Bombay-Poona route of the Central Railway. It was not built by the British but was an unusual enterprise for an Indian business czar, Sir Adamjee Peerbhoy, a wealthy cotton merchant. His son, Abdul Hussain, convinced the Dawoodi Bohra entrepreneur – he was a major supplier of canvas tents to the British army – to support this venture. The Peerbhoys had been frequent visitors to the small hill station of Matheran which was, as the crow flies, a mere 30 miles east of Bombay. However, it was not easy to get to and initially, Sir Adamjee had a *kutcha* road (more like a dirt track) carved out of the hillside to connect Neral to Matheran. It was used by enthusiastic trekkers, those on horseback and of course by *palki*-borne visitors.

Better connectivity was clearly in order, and after his father gave him the green signal, Abdul Hussain utilised the expertise of a Punjabi engineer to survey the area for the laying of the railway track. In 1904, Hussain camped at Neral to plan and supervise the work that started on his pet scheme; the two feet gauge line running over a distance of 12 miles and travelling at the same speed as it climbed almost 3,000 feet was opened to traffic in 1907. The project that had cost Rs 16 lakh – a huge sum in those days – was completed in fourteen months, a record of sorts. However, by the time that Oliver wrote her handy little book, the popularity of Matheran among the rulers had declined; Kashmir was increasingly a favoured destination as were the 'Neilgherries' (Nilgiris). As the British moved on, increasingly affluent Indians found the small hill station attractive, buying up properties and putting down roots in what were usually second homes. The unique railway certainly helped in the process of Indianisation of an initially 'white' space.

'Sri Aurobindo Ghosh and the Mother at Darshan'
From the album 'Sri Aurobindo and his Ashram' *by Henri Cartier-Bresson*

PONDICHERRY
IN BLACK AND WHITE

⟳

Two thousand and eleven was the centenary year of The Historical Society of French India (La Société d'Histoire de l'Inde Française). It was founded by the French governor of Pondicherry, Alfred Martineau, with the intention of bringing together archival papers dealing with this French enclave. Among Martineau's significant finds was the forgotten *Les Mémoires de François Martin* (The Memoirs of François Martin), discovered among papers stored at the National Archives in Paris. Martin founded Pondicherry in 1674, became its first governor-general and set up the French East India Company; his writings have been translated by scholar Lotika Varadarajan as *India in the 17th Century, Social, Economic and Political: Memoirs of François Martin, 1670-1694*.

Trade based on the fine cloth woven from the cotton in the hinterland was a major attraction; initial settlers were the Portuguese in 1521, followed by the Danes, the Dutch and then following a brief spell under the British, Pondicherry was finally ceded to the French in 1826. With a past so intermeshed with different cultural and subcultural influences, Pondicherry could hardly be anything but a space of vibrant growth. Historically, the town was divided into the European section and the larger Indian part, the two being separated by a canal. In no time, European influences led to a unique synergy in architectural styles, cultural practices and cuisines.

By the final decades of the 19th century, photography arrived in the region, and a recent publication of the Alkazi Collection of Photography (*Mastering the Lens – Before and After Cartier-Bresson in Pondicherry*) carries some early images of the area. There is a broad street in Karical (present-day Karaikal, within the Union territory of Pondicherry and a bit more than a 100 kilometres from the city), various imposing buildings such as Government House, Messages Maritime (post office) and others. Apart from those taken by the Bourne & Shepherd stable, there are some striking landscape format images attributed to a C. Moyne, who photographed panoramas as well as the lighthouse, temples and the cathedral.

While it did not have a studio in Madras, the management of Bourne & Shepherd possibly found it worthwhile to send a team to the town to photograph a little beyond the now somewhat common 'Views of India' images: with studios in Calcutta, Simla and Bombay, it was perhaps not too difficult to dispatch skilled photographers with attendant staff, heavy equipment and a clear mandate to photograph the somewhat more unusual in a region beyond the purview of the Raj. There are two most fascinating photographs by what was then perhaps India's leading studio: one of the coastline from the sea and another of the unique mode of transportation, the Railka, also known as 'La Pondicherienne', the 'push-push or street conveyance'. The title of the coastline image reads, 'Pondicherry from the Sea' and in the foreground are small rowing boats of the kind that ferried passengers from bigger liners to the shore. It is possible that the image was taken by one such boat on a calm day.

Of far greater interest is the photograph of the Railka; with a comfortable seat not unlike that of a brougham beneath a fringed canopy, it had four wheels and a most unusual steering apparatus to be operated by the passenger. As it was pushed from the back, there clearly had to be communication between the passenger and the 'pushers'. All this, of course, is in the realm of conjecture, but a vehicle of this kind can hardly not lead to thoughts on how people interact and cultures meld, borrow or reject even at the level of transportation.

'Railka: Pondicherry'
Photograph by Bourne & Shepherd studios, c. 1890s

Architecture, particularly domestic architecture, became the most visible and dominant example of an interface between different styles. French homes had high ceilings, arched doorways, and if more than one storey, vaulted staircases. These occupied pride of place along the coast and near Government House. Though Tamil homes retained their own distinctive features with a public veranda along the street (*thalvaram*) and the *thinnai*, a semi-private veranda with seating areas for visitors who were not usually to be invited into the inner quarters, there were homes that also adopted aspects of French architecture; arched doorways and fluted pilasters were particularly striking features of this peculiar Franco-Tamil architectural style.

It was to this town that Cambridge-educated Aurobindo Ghosh came in 1910, having given up politics following his exoneration in the Alipur bomb case. For the next forty years he devoted himself to spiritual practice and yoga; in 1926, with Mirra Alfassa, whom he named the Mother, he established Aurobindo Ashram. Their spiritual collaboration attracted many devotees and with the Mother's astute guidance and entrepreneurial acumen, educational institutions, artistic creativity and photography soon found space to flourish. It is not surprising then that Henri Cartier-Bresson, who had first come to India to photograph Mahatma Gandhi's funeral in 1948, wrote asking to be allowed to take images of *darshan*, where, four times in the year, Sri Aurobindo and the Mother appeared before their devotees; he would also document life in the ashram. As Sri Aurobindo rarely allowed photographers, when permission was granted, it was a coup of sorts. Apart from the image of Sri Aurobindo and the Mother at *darshan* on April 24, 1950, there are several of daily rituals at the ashram: the Mother receiving devotees, throwing flowers to them, and a particularly interesting series of her playing tennis wearing a white salwar kameez. Cartier-Bresson was allowed access to Sri Aurobindo's room and a carefully angled shot from the side of the bed focuses on the tiger skin draped across it, writing desk with a few books, open window and a door beyond. In his personal diary, the photographer obviously could not but help comment on 'the inevitable tiger skin which seems the companion of those aiming at spiritual achievement.' All negatives and prints of the photo shoot were acquired by the Mother and a selection became part of a limited edition album; this became of historical and sentimental significance as Sri Aurobindo died a few months after, at the age of seventy-eight.

The camera was not new to Pondicherry; in the 1940s, photography was introduced to the ashram by Nairobi-trained Chimanbhai Patel who set up the Photo Service, complete with a darkroom and an enlarger. 'Ashram Photography' became the name officially assigned to photography from the studio and about the time that Cartier-Bresson arrived for his shoot, Pranab Kumar Bhattacharya and Tara Jauhar had started visually documenting life and work at the ashram. These two photographers along with Venkatesh Shirodkar took art images in black and white – unusual portraits, figures in silhouette, chiaroscuros of shimmering waters and so on.

Perhaps inspired by Cartier-Bresson's visit and the Mother's evident interest in photography, the Pondicherry international photography exhibition was organised by photographer Robi Ganguli; clearly as over two dozen countries participated, Pondicherry had become a familiar

Photograph of Calvé College, c. 1920s
A good example of architectural syncretism, it is now a government school

locale for photographic aficionados. A viewing of the images that are now available make clear that photography at Aurobindo Ashram played much more than an instrumental role: for, as a one-time artist trained at Ecole des Beaux-Arts, Paris, the Mother believed that 'photography is an art when the photographer is an artist'. Her view found ample testimony in the work of a handful of creative photographers who were able to combine an artistic sensibility with dexterity behind the lens.

'Madras from the Pier'
Photograph by Wiele & Klien studio, 1910

SURF, SAND
AND
COURTYARDS

⌒⤚

On December 21, 2006, Chennai Port – earlier known as Madras Harbour – celebrated the 125th year of its existence. In 1884, three years after the opening of the Harbour, Governor Mountstuart Elphinstone Grant Duff built the promenade along the beach and named it Madras Marina. He proudly announced that 'the rather dismal beach of five years ago' was now 'one of the most beautiful promenades in the world'.

The history of Madras, of course, is much older – the city commemorated its 350th anniversary in 1989. On St. George's Day (April 23, 1640) Francis Day, a factor of the East India Company, who had earlier negotiated a land grant with a representative of the waning Vijayanagar Empire, his boss Cogan and local *dubashes*, christened the fortified factory they had built, 'Fort St. George'. This was in the little fishing village called Madraspatnam, discovered by the British in 1639, that was gradually to gain in prominence by the early part of the 18th century. By then, the Company was active on the Coromandel Coast and Madras became a gracious town, and later a city where the British tried out various architectural styles.

Fort St. George. Photograph, c. 1920s

In time, its coastline was developed, pioneering educational institutions established and in 1792, an observatory was set up. As the first port city in India, it became an important naval base as well as an administrative centre of the growing British dominions in southern India. However, until well into the 19th century, ships were anchored about a quarter mile offshore and passengers had to climb down into *masula* boats with flimsy catamarans in attendance; their skilled crew were in a constant state of preparedness in case they had to rescue any hapless passengers who might have the misfortune to fall into the water. Cargo to and from larger vessels was transported in a similarly unconventional manner. The planks of these flexible *masula* boats were sewn together with coir rope and to enable them to withstand the pressure of the surf, they had no frames or ribs.

Sea journeys to this coast were clearly treacherous. In the 1820s, Bishop Heber travelled from Calcutta to Madras by sea, and he, as well as Albert Hervey, a cadet in the Madras army, commented on the phenomenal surf near the shore. Hervey wrote in 1832: 'Everybody has heard or read of the famous Madras surf – that tremendous barrier which guards the shores of the coast, so replete with danger to the uninitiated; and those dreadful sharks which swarm outside ready to pounce upon any unfortunate victim who may fall into the water ... in crossing the surf some degree of skill is necessary to strand boats in safety, and the boatmen usually demand a present for a job, for which they are already well paid.' Bishop Heber's journey, however, was quite uneventful – though he too made a mention of the dreaded surf – 'the contrary wind that had so long delayed us, ensured us a peaceful landing, as it blew directly off shore'. As the loss of cargo during such brief but tricky forays was not unknown, quite clearly some better arrangement had to be made. Though Warren Hastings had thought about a harbour in 1770, it took over a century for the first masonry breakwaters to be constructed on the suggestion of a Mr Parkes of Karachi Harbour fame. Cyclones with almost the force of tsunamis were not unusual, and one in 1881 badly damaged the newly built port when 'half a mile of the breakwaters (each was 3,000 feet long)' were washed away.

The port catered to a fast-growing trade and passenger traffic while the coastline developed into beaches. Commenting on early 20th-century Madras, K.P.S. Menon, an early member of the ICS, wrote in his travelogue, *Journey Round the World*, 'what we enjoyed most of all was an evening on the beach. Where in the wide world can you see such a spacious beach with such silky sand? But its character has changed since my days as a college student in the Madras Christian College [established in 1837] during the First World War. Then it was almost an exclusive resort for English or Anglicized gentlemen'. Scores of horse-drawn carriages and a few cars used to draw up in the evenings where 'on certain days, an English band would play English music for English children'.

Architectural innovation played itself out in Chepauk Palace, the Central Station, Senate House, Victoria Hall and so on. According to a well-known chronicler of the city, S. Muthiah, it was Robert Chisholm, first principal of the Madras School of Industrial Art and consulting architect to the government of Madras, who changed the city's skyline. He introduced the Indo-Saracenic form where the Hindu and Islamic blended with Gothic revival: cupolas, domes and arches melded with the fine lines of European buildings. Domestic architecture flourished through bungalows that combined deep verandas leading on to central rooms, a kitchen at the

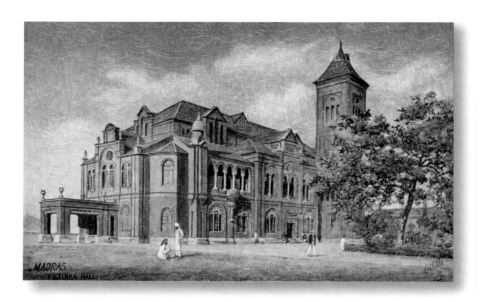

'Madras. Victoria Hall.'
Postcard by Raphael Tuck & Sons, 1905

back and servants' quarters at the far end of the compound. In their 1883 bible for wives and homemakers, *The Complete Indian Housekeeper and Cook*, Flora Annie Steel and Grace Gardiner noted approvingly that 'the Madras Presidency is distinctly a cheap place to live in.' Beef sold for 6 annas a seer (2 pounds) and eggs were 3 or 4 annas a dozen. Within the Presidency, 'a nice house could be rented for between Rs 50 to Rs 100'. Life, they noted, was 'more Oriental in its ways' than in other parts of the country. In part, this possibly meant that the core of Tamilian society maintained its intrinsic values – even the brown sahibs of the bureaucracy, trade, commerce and learning rarely forgot the fundamentals of Carnatic culture and tradition.

The structure and interior of bungalows and houses of the indigenous elite reflected this ability to balance cultural influences – perhaps most pronounced among the mercantilist Chettiars. It is in the districts of Ramnad and Pudukkottai that an interesting combination of the West and indigenous domestic architecture finds expression in the homes of the Naattukottai Chettiars (Chettiars who live in country forts). Not far from

Madurai is Karaikudi, known as the capital of the Chettinad region, a city dotted with mansions of this affluent community. The Chettiars can trace their roots to 10th-century traders from inscriptions in Ramnad district, and from the middle of the 19th century till Independence, Naattukottai Chettiars were the bankers of Southeast Asia. They were highly successful in Ceylon, Burma, Indo-China, Sumatra, Mauritius, Singapore and Malaysia. Expectedly, houses became mansions and grew in style, size and opulence as their owners prospered under the British.

The external veranda of these homes that abutted on the street was predominantly a male space, separated from the interior by huge Burma teak doors, elaborately carved or even inlaid with Belgian mirrors and Italian tiles. Before one got to the *muttram* within, there were two more smaller, raised verandas where women spent much of their time. And of course, as with havelis and courtyard houses in other parts of the country, this was the private domain. Elaborate columns supported a narrower veranda that ran round the courtyard from which led off the family rooms. Marriages were conducted in this central space, and contracts as well were signed here – the need for privacy while negotiating such deals necessitated the opening up of this private area to outsiders.

Many generations lived within these homes, and life-cycle rituals were events of great splendour and sumptuousness. All this started changing after Independence. As with many other communities, younger generations migrated and many homes today are empty, if not neglected. However, to cater to a growing local tourist traffic curious about an India they know so little about as well as to those from abroad, a few of the more enterprising Chettiars have converted homes into heritage sites. These are open to visitors, and often family members and old retainers welcome them, and, if they are lucky, they are served choice items of the famed Chettinad cuisine!

General view of Madras taken from the lighthouse
Photograph, c. 1920s

'Madras. Senate House.'
Postcard by Raphael Tuck & Sons, 1910

FROM A 'PEPPER POT'
TO AN
ICE HOUSE

⤙

*B*lending a keen travel writer's eye with ethnographic perceptions, Jan Morris describes British architecture in India as being 'slightly mutated *en voyage*'. She comments on what she felt were the skewed architectural aesthetics of the British in India: the Grecian, Gothic and the Baroque were 'cluttered with devices against the weather' and porticoes and verandas were blocked with rattan screens, while shutters and hoods shaded windows. The more innovative and adaptive learnt to utilise chiaroscuros; the 'less skilled merely shoved on an extra verandah here, projecting eaves there, giving their work, all too often, an air of slightly hangdog makeshift'. Morris' rather damning critique of colonial architecture was perhaps aimed at the flurry of architectural enthusiasm in the three presidencies.

While Calcutta and Bombay were clearly at the forefront of colonial building activity, Madras was a slow third, with much emphasis on its waterfront: Morris writes that at the start of the 19th century, for those arriving in the city from the water, it was as though they were 'approaching a foreshore lined with Grecian temples'; at the end of the century, 'it was like sailing into some fantasy of orientalism'. A fantasy that 'fused Eastern and Western aesthetics', writes Shanti Jayewardene-Pillai. She reminds us that unlike the other two presidency capitals, Madras was home to a native king who regarded the East India Company not as his equal but rather his servant; this factor, Jayewardene-Pillai believes, led to its 'peculiar architectural culture'. Those Indians and colonials involved in designing and constructing the many buildings of Madras, were, she writes, the Indo-Britons; the product of their efforts, of course, represents the apogee of Indo-Saracenic architecture. The construction of the sea wall round the heavily guarded Fort St. George as well as that of the sewers in the Black Town required knowledge of local conditions and materials – an expertise that was easily available with Indians enlisted for the job. A port city till well into the 19th century, Madras consisted of the walled Black Town of 'native' settlements. To its south was the Fort and beyond stood Chepauk Palace, home to the Nawabs of Carnatic. They patronised a Muslim courtly culture and had well-known Sufi scholar-mystics as guests.

While there were some feeble attempts at bringing about an interface between cultures through, for instance the Cosmopolitan Club, Jayewardene-Pillai argues that it was the dynamism of the governor, Francis Napier, that led to 'a peculiar and unexpected hybrid imperial architectural style'. And Robert Chisholm was the man chosen to design and implement the construction of many of these buildings.

In the 1860s, when the government of Madras launched a competition for the best plans for Presidency College and the Senate House of the university, seventeen proposals were received; the judges decided on the designs of Robert Chisholm, an executive engineer in Bengal's Public Works' Department. In no time, Chisholm became a favourite of Governor Napier, who soon asked for him to be appointed as consulting architect to the Madras government. This was not an easy request to accede to and Napier had to work hard to convince the viceroy of Chisholm's indispensability. By 1870, the well-paid Chisholm was designing the museum, telegraph office, jail and *cutcherry* offices. A year earlier, on a direct brief from the governor, he had submitted designs for the university's Senate House. Its four 'pepper-pot minarets' (Morris) clearly represented a syncretist vision

Santhome Basilica. Photograph, c. 1920s
In 1839 the British rebuilt the original Portuguese structure in Neo-Gothic style

and Jayewardene-Pillai feels that the Byzantian inspiration for the building came from Napier who had lived in Istanbul; while Chisholm agreed that he was influenced by Byzantine, he ruefully concluded that the building had 'no particular style' at all. His view is shared by Jayewardene-Pillai who feels that it 'defies comfortable classification'.

If the Santhome Basilica and Senate House is a must-see for architecturally inclined visitors to Chennai today, so is Ice House: this two-storeyed building with its rounded frontage, elegant verandas and classical arches is indeed a curiosity. It is also a house with a history that reflects in ample measure the hybridity of its appearance: how many buildings of yore can claim to be an ice store, host to Swami Vivekananda and then home to Brahmin widows?

In 1997, the sadly dilapidated Ice House was finally gifted to the Ramakrishna Mission – always the wish of its one-time owner, Bilagiri Iyengar. The house was originally leased from the government in 1845 by a New England entrepreneur, Frederic Tudor, whose penchant for cold drinks led him to an unusual worldwide trade. Ice blocks were brought from Boston by clipper and stored in this quaint building till the 1870s.

According to S. Muthiah, who has written widely on the British in Madras, the ownership of Ice House passed to the advocate, Bilagiri Iyengar, who renamed it Castle Kernan after a judge of the Madras High Court. In February 1897, Swami Vivekananda visited the house on his return from his highly successful tour of the West. Shortly afterwards, the southern chapter of the Ramakrishna movement was founded within the gracious rooms of the Castle.

In 1912, it required the enterprising and unconventional Sister Subbalakshmi to choose such an unusual locale for her wards, young Brahmin widows. Ignoring many raised eyebrows, she was willing to take on the ghosts that supposedly haunted the building and local fisherfolk, who offered to do a puja to propitiate restless spirits, were politely shown the door. Despite an initial visitation by a snake, strange noises and shadows, the girls settled quite happily. It had been a long road for the eleven-year-old child widow whose parents not only supported her desire to be educated but also had refused to have Subbalakshmi's head tonsured or put her in widows' weeds. Instead, they helped their Madras Presidency College-educated daughter to set up a home for young widows whose education could not be supported by their families.

Soon, there were over seventy girls in Ice House, and in 1920, Sister Subbalakshmi was awarded the Kaiser-i-Hind for her commitment to a disprivileged group. By now she had started a school for children from fisher families and also accepted young women who wanted to defer marriage. All, however, had to be Brahmins and Subbalakshmi resisted the suggestion of the reformist doctor, Muthulakshmi Reddy to admit the daughters of *devadasis* (dancers attached to Hindu temples). Though the Sister's resistance to admit the daughters of 'DGs' (dancing girls) to the home was a reflection of dominant upper-caste sentiment, radical changes in thinking were in the offing. In 1925, E. V. Ramasamy (also known as Periyar) started the Self-Respect Movement which called upon the backward castes to challenge the diktats of a caste-based social order. She however, remained unmoved.

Ironically, a decade later, Rukmini Devi Arundale took Madras by storm when she danced at the Diamond Jubilee Convention of the Theosophical Society. The new dance form – Bharat Natyam – had roots in the *devadasi*

*Photograph of
Rukmini Devi Arundale,
c. 1940s*

tradition. In 1936, together with her husband, George Arundale, Rukmini established Kalakshetra, that popularised Bharat Natyam.

An abiding conundrum remains: buildings that survive from the Raj are often the product of many diverse – if not competing – architectural traditions. What is less known is that these hybrids have, over time, been homes to persons who might never have normally met nor interacted with each other. If, as in the case of Ice House, one is able to unearth a lineage of residents, an interesting matrix of the colonial interface emerges. One that would lead us to ask how would Sister Subbalakshmi have reacted if she chanced upon the swashbuckling Frederic Tudor supervising the unloading of his cargo of ice on the lonely beach? Would she throw up her hands in alarm, as she did at the thought of DG inmates? Or would she accept it as one of the ironies of history?

'*The Rajah of Putteealla*'
Hand-coloured lithograph in Portraits of the Princes & Peoples of India
by Emily Eden (1797–1869)

Wanderings
of a
Pilgrim
and
Others

A dak peon. Photograph, c. 1920s

A SHORT HISTORY
OF THE
TRAVELLING EYE

*I*n pre-1850s India, people on the move were significant reminders of class and caste differences: those better placed in life used various modes of transportation – some were borne to their destinations in *palkis* on the shoulders of strong young men, most often from the lower castes. Others used animal-drawn carts and carriages and even boats and rafts. The majority of Indians however, walked – often long distances, the *dak* runner being a case in point. Pandita Ramabai, one of India's first women social reformers, and probably among the most controversial women of her times, writes that 'for three years after the death of our parents and eldest sister we [Ramabai and her brother] walked more than 4000 miles on foot without any sort of comfort'. Born in 1858 into an impoverished Chitpavan Brahmin family of Poona (Pune) – her father, Ananta Shastri Dongre, was a priest committed to the education of women – Ramabai learned Sanskrit early. When the intrepid teenage pair undertook their long trek, it is likely that they supported themselves by interpreting the scriptures as they traversed India.

For the more daring, horses were indispensable across lonely terrains, inhospitable deserts and on the battlefield; Rana Pratap's Chetak remains an icon in the mythology of human-animal relations; and who knows what Rani Lakshmibai of Jhansi's fate would have been in the battle for Gwalior in February 1857 if her faithful steed who was mortally wounded had not been replaced by a younger, less experienced one? The increasingly complicated business of the Raj, families on the move, the occasional joyride, all depended on trusted animals. Horse-drawn carts, carriages, and of course the worthy bullock cart that remains an abiding counterpoint to many a Mercedes or BMW on dust-laden Indian roads — have a long history.

Among the more fragile cargo that bullock carts were entrusted with was tons of photographic gear not only of individual entrepreneurs such as Raja Deen Dayal and Samuel Bourne but also of Linnaeus Tripe, an officer of the 12th Madras Native Infantry. Nothing less than four bullock carts transported equipment and his staff on a journey that was to cover Salem, Srirangam, Trichy, Madurai, Pudukkottai and Tanjore and finally Madras.

Till well into the 19th century, travel was often fraught with danger and security of person and goods was a very real issue in the Indian countryside. In riverine India, waterborne locomotion was common — but the fear of dacoity in these pre-steamer days was a distinct possibility. Country boats used to be attacked at night by dacoits wielding flaming *mashals*. While Reginald Heber, the bishop of Calcutta, baulked at the size of a modest entourage of three elephants, over twenty camels, five horses and several ponies, he knew that he had no option. His extensive tour of India involved tug and steamer rides as well as the services of several animals. As he went on, a number of small traders and others, believing in safety in numbers, asked to join the large party and 'travel under our protection'. Living under canvas for long stretches was not unknown, often necessitated by the nature of the work of the civil servant, judge, surveyor and explorer.

The memoirs of both Indian and European women have interesting insights into travel — as well as a clear admission that without the protection of the Raj, Englishwomen would hardly have the freedom to traverse India, often on their own. In *A Month in a Dandi — A Woman's Wanderings in Northern India* (1891) Christina Bremner wrote that 'the safety of a single

Plate VIII.

Head of the Glacier.

Nanda-kot, 22,500 Ft.

GLACIER OF THE PINDAR, 12,000 Feet.
Published by Smith, Elder & C? London.

'Glacier of the Pindar, 12,000 Feet.'
Hand-coloured lithograph of a surveyor's camp, c. 1850s

traveller depends on the goodwill of villagers and on the length of England's right arm'. She described *dandis* at length and was quick to point out that they catered to those willing to brave the mountains in hammock-like slings carried by sturdy coolies. Though historian, David Arnold feels that after the middle of the 19th century, writing on travel had become as clichéd 'as a palanquin', only to be brilliantly revived by Kipling, the gaze from what Emily Eden called 'beds in boxes' soon provided interesting insights on early colonial India. When Governor-General Auckland's entourage of 12,000 moved from Calcutta to the Upper Provinces in 1837, the variety in the mode of travel was indeed impressive: after an initial riverine journey, elephants and humans carried men, women and pets in howdahs, palanquins, *doolies, dandis* and *jhampans*, while horses drew carriages, hackneys, tongas, carts and buggies.

'View at Simla. 1825.'

This interesting lithograph of Simla depicts various forms of locomotion used at the time. A sahib on horseback is crossing a bridge while below to the left, coolies rest besides a *jhampan*; a bullock cart trundles into the frame at the right

The fearless Fanny Parkes, a contemporary of the Eden sisters (and apparently a more likeable personality), who had joined the imperial entourage for a while commented that 'it is said his Lordship's marching about the country costs the Government 70,000 rupees a month'. For most of her journey, however, Fanny did not have the protective umbrella of the Raj at first hand: earlier, in December 1834, eager to accept this country with all its spots and warts, sailed from Allahabad to Agra on a journey of fifty-one days with a crew of twenty-one – and her pet terrier. Fanny Parkes wrote of her more adventurous travels with gleeful delight: in December 1834, her night-time journey in a *palki* up to Landowr (Landour) in Mussooree (Mussoorie), when 'we passed through a forest or *sal jangal* as they call it',

MEMORIES OF BELONGING

also included an encounter with a tiger lying by the wayside. Though the bearers put down their palanquin, and 'howled and screamed with all their might', as the big cat moved off, Fanny got out of the palanquin 'to look at a tiger *au naturel*'. On that fine and clear moonlit night, 'the *jangal* looked well and its interest was heightened by the idea that you might now and then see a wild beast'. On her long travels, Fanny used every possible mode of transport available in those days.

As animals tire easily, when traversing the countryside, a relay system was devised, particularly for the carrying of mail or *dak*. If there was space, a traveller could book his seat in any palanquin, boat, horse, coach or cart carrying mail and parcel – that is, if a runner was not carrying the post. The post or *dak* runner is a part of colonial folklore and the potentially dangerous journey meant considerable *bandobast*. Each *dak* runner was provided with a drummer in forest tracts, besides an escort of two torchbearers and two archers after nightfall. C.A. Bayly writes of the tense months in 1857, when the fall of Delhi was reported to the authorities in Firozpur by official runners; as carriages, carts and waterborne vessels of all kinds – including inflatable animals skins – were used not only for travel but also for conveying important information by the so-called 'rebels', these were quickly seized by the chief commissioner of Punjab.

It was while on his travels that Bishop Heber died in Trichinopoly (Tiruchirapalli) in 1826, supposedly of apoplexy after a cold water bath. The lithograph overleaf, based on a detailed engraving of an event that must surely have been a shock to many, is an artist's account not only of the death but also of the multifarious activities surrounding British life in India. The bishop is being carried into a house, presumably that of Mr Bird, circuit judge with whom he was staying, by two white men, one of whom (in top hat and boots) may be a doctor or an apothecary. An excited 'native' leads the way. Of interest are the various structures, including a gazebo-like building and a marquee that might have been the bathing tent where Heber died. A large retinue of attendants and some sepoys are standing around. At the right-hand corner a man is smoking a hookah, apparently unmindful of the events round him. There is considerable activity as well as confusion in the image – and a sense of people having been on the

'The Death of Bishop Heber'
Lithograph based on a drawing by H. Melville and engraved by J. Sands

move. In the background are elephants with howdahs, men on horseback, and in the right-hand corner, what appears to be a bed with an elaborate caparisoned top. It could also be a variant of the upper-class *jhampan*. In pre-photography days, the artist would have had the freedom to embellish his image with flights of fancy. Of significance is that various modes of locomotion have also been represented in what should have been a sombre portrayal of a sudden and tragic death of a man as eminent as Bishop Heber. It only confirms that in the 18th and 19th centuries, travel was a significant feature of life, often stressful and usually with adventures of kind or another.

A FAMILY
ON THE MOVE

~~~

*I*ndians have been peripatetic for centuries, travelling both within the country and abroad, and with British rule, employment-related middle-class migration picked up. Some planned their ventures meticulously, often following family members who had made good in the growing urban areas; for others, dramatic serendipity was instrumental in the undertaking of long journeys away from home. When he was a young man of seventeen, Harcharan Bandyopadhyay – father of the Christian preacher, Kalicharan Bandyopadhyay, and grandfather of Brahmabandhab Upadhyay – was spotted by Major Sleeman, the infamous 'slayer of thugs', as he bravely beat to death a snake that had ventured into the former's tent. This was in Hooghly district, around 1829, where Sleeman had pitched camp. Close to a century later, Harcharan's daughter, Nistarini Debi, recounted the incident to her biographer in *Sekeley Katha* (An Old-fashioned Tale); she was unlettered and it is possible that she was persuaded to speak about her life because the chronicler-nephew was interested in knowing more about some eminent men in her family.

Sleeman sahib had known zamindar Rammohan, Harcharan's father-in-law, and hearing of the young lad's hard times, appointed him an assistant writer. Soon, 'seating him in the palanquin carrying injured soldiers, he took

Harcharan away with him'. Sleeman was on a constant lookout for well-built young men with a penchant for adventure, who would find hunting down thugs a worthwhile occupation. The handsome Harcharan fitted the bill, and when, by the mid-1830s, Sleeman's anti-thuggee operations were responsible for covering a large part of north and central India, he found a niche for himself in the growing bureaucratic structure at Jubbalpore (Jabalpur). While some have argued that thugs were no different from other criminals and that thuggee did not exist, others cite Sleeman's impressive database of records based on genealogies, testaments, village histories, maps and cartographic visuals to prove that thuggee was different from other forms of criminality.

Those revisiting the phenomenon of organised terror of a subject people against itself describe the thugs' depredations and commitment to chiefly bloodless murder by strangulation; their distinctive modus operandi was to kill before committing robbery. While reliable figures are difficult to come by, Mike Dash feels that the thugs killed about 50,000 men, women and children at a minimum – much less than the fanciful estimates of Sleeman and others.

Whatever the truth about thugs may be, Harcharan rose rapidly in the hierarchy, though for months his perturbed family did not know where he had disappeared to. He soon became a favourite of the Major sahib and when his monthly salary went up to thirty rupees, he contacted his family who were 'delighted at the thought of seeing money'. His moment of glory came when he was transferred to Chhapra in Bihar from the headquarters at Jubbalpore. Nistarini describes his path to success in detail. He was assigned the task of ridding the river of the crocodile menace as well as dealing with thugs. If any woman got into the river with jewels, crocodiles would carry her off; her dead body would be found floating later. Nothing would happen to the men. Harcharan surmised that this was not the work of crocodiles but of thugs. One day, he put on a woman's clothes and jewels and tied a rope around his waist. Instructing two persons to hold on to the free end of the rope while standing at the bank, he got into the water. As soon as he did so, something appeared to be pulling him away into the deep. Harcharan then signalled to those waiting by pulling at the rope and caught hold of his aggressor. When he reached the shore, everyone saw that Harcharan had dragged along a thug. The minute he let him go, a crowd collected. 'Seeing no option, the fellow tried to look downcast and ashamed'; but Harcharan landed the man a mighty slap ... 'and the thug fell down with that one blow. This incident paved the way for Baba's success in the future' (*Sekeley Katha*).

An elated Harcharan now moved to Gorakhpur, and brought his two wives with their children to join him. Nistarini was born there around 1832 and also spent her early years in the town. Travelling considerable distances became a part of the family's life, and when a suitable bridegroom who fitted the requirements of their sub-caste, that of *kulin* Brahmins, could not be found for Nistarini in the areas that Harcharan was familiar with, he decided that she should be sent back to the ancestral village, Khanyan, in Hooghly district. Together with 'my two mothers', three sisters and three brothers, including the two-year-old Kalicharan, the family and its entourage of attendants started the long journey. This was in the 1840s: 'there were no railways in those days. What takes a day today took us a full month'. The party arrived in the Vindyachal region in three or four oxen-drawn tongas and changed into boats at Varanasi. When they reached Tribeni, a place of pilgrimage in the northern most part of Bansberia town, it was the palanquin-bearers' turn to take over for the final leg to Khanyan.

A much-married older man was found for Nistarini, who was over fourteen at the time of her marriage. However, she continued to live with her own family and commented that 'I had hardly seen my husband's face'. In keeping with *kulin* traditions, her husband had no fixed home, travelling as he did among the houses of his many wives, collecting whatever he could for his survival as he went along. Much of Nistarini's life appeared to have been punctuated by travel, as she too had to divide her time between her parents' home and, later, those of various male relatives. The women surely maintained purdah, but it is possible that for a family of migrants whose women had, by compulsion, a certain amount of exposure to the world beyond, the strict norms of upper-caste society were not always feasible.

By her middle years, Nistarini was familiar with all modes of transportation, including train journeys on the newly opened line with her youngest nephew, Tarini Charan, who had got a job in the Morse office of

'Palanquin and Women'
Lithograph based on a two-part painting commissioned from Indian artists
by the French engraver and printer, Firmin Didot, 1805

the railways at Halisahar. Her younger brother, Kalicharan – a protégé of the missionary and educationist, Alexander Duff, and later a well-respected Christian preacher – supported Nistarini financially as well as emotionally, even to the extent of encouraging her to live in a room alone in Calcutta when oppression by her sisters-in-law became unbearable.

Two of Harcharan's grandsons chose to run away – but unlike their grandfather, travel did not bring them much success. However, it did bring accolades and fame to Bhawani, his eldest grandson, later known as Brahmabandhab Upadhyay, who died in 1907. A controversial figure, he became a Catholic who also preached Vedanta, called himself a Hindu Catholic and would attend Annie Besant's lectures on theosophy – and then proceed to give counter-lectures. But not before he had been through a phase with the Brahmo Samaj, led by Keshub Sen, and travelled all the way to Hyderabad in Sind (now in Pakistan) to teach at a school. This was in 1888. Three years later, he became a Catholic. Like Harcharan, Brahmabandhab travelled to Jubbalpore for an unusual form of employment: he established a short-lived *kasthalika matha* or a Catholic monastery, whose aim was to Indianise all the teachings of Christianity. Not unexpectedly, this did not meet with the approval of the order – although he continued to teach there for a few years, keeping alive the family's connections with central India. Finally, he became an ardent nationalist, working with Rabindranath Tagore on the establishment of Santiniketan.

When being shared among her relatives became too tiring and stressful for Nistarini, she agreed to go away to Kashi (Varanasi) and live on her own. Unlike most other upper-caste widows, she did not join an ashram but chose to live on her own. Her family visited her off and on, and it was here that she dictated her reminiscences, by the light of a small kerosene lantern. By then, her eyes were rheumy and weak. But one can imagine them lighting up as she recounted the several and varied journeys and escapades of this interesting family – one of a growing number for whom migration and travel became the route to employment and upward mobility.

Cabinet-size portrait of Kamala Bose
by Bourne & Shepherd studios, c. 1890s

THE FEMALE GAZE

*A*fter the middle of the 19th century, when upper- and middle-
class Indian women started leaving their homes for social events
or even for a visit to the photographic studio, the occasions
required considerable organisation and arrangement: in many parts of the
country, the requirements of purdah meant that initially the closed *palki* and
later the more exclusive broughams and landaus with curtains were used. For
the less affluent, the bullock cart was also used in an innovative manner by
women in purdah: in the photograph of a 'shrouded' bullock cart in a town
in central India (overleaf), the women passengers are completely concealed
from view. They are seated beneath the dome fabricated from wood and
bamboo covered with a heavy canvas-like material, surely unbearable in
a hot climate. Nevertheless, this suffocating mode of transportation had
clearly passed the test of privacy, enabling protection from the male gaze.

In the early part of the 20th century, Sister Subbalakshmi, who was to
become the first widow graduate of Madras, went to study at Presidency
College in a rickshaw with its hood pulled right down. In addition, she
would open her large, black umbrella and hold it in front of her like a
protective shield. All that could be seen of her from the outside was the
brightly coloured border of her sari. While she did not observe purdah,
decorum required that Subbalakshmi should remain 'invisible' to curious

A 'shrouded' bullock cart in central India. Photograph, c. 1900s

eyes. Descriptions of travel occupy considerable space in women's memoirs and letters – they write of riverine sojourns, of being carried in *palkis*, *jhampans* and *doolies*, oxen and horse-drawn tonga and bullock cart rides, and a few mention train journeys.

Travel was often necessitated by certain middle-class lifestyles of fathers and, later, of husbands. Among the more unusual were *shikar* trips and camp life – the former a part of acquired upper middle-class leisure time activity, while going to camp was de rigueur for members of the civil service, the growing tribe of archaeologists, ethnographers, scientists, geologists and so on. Such excursions involved considerable *bandobast* with subsidiary tents for cooks, *khalasis*, *khitmadgars*, *jamadars* as is clear from many accounts of life at camp. Lady Lyle Maxwell toured widely with her husband, Reginald who was in the Indian Civil Service (ICS). Posted in the North Kanara district of Bombay Presidency, their touring life started in November and ended in March. In the forests, a little complex of canvas would soon appear as within hours a living room, bedroom, 'necessary tents' and an office tent were pitched by the efficient touring staff. Stores were carried in large wooden boxes lined with kerosene tins. Lady Lyle had some sympathy for the servants who she felt had a hard and somewhat unpredictable life while at camp: if they met with adventure during the search for campsites, the pitching of tents were a casualty – when for instance, 'wild elephants may be heard and frighten the bullocks, or tigers and panthers be about'. Campsites could be idyllic where the 'jungles looked like a fairyland at night, and from my bed I looked through the tent door right into the forest all lit up by the moon'. Or they could well be unpleasant, leech-ridden, sodden and uncomfortable.

Almost half a century before Lady Maxwell's description of the enchanted jungle, Kamala and Pramatha Nath Bose had spent many months in the heart of India. Bose was a pioneering geologist, and his work entailed prospecting in diverse terrains. Within a few months of her marriage in 1882, sixteen-year-old Kamala was preparing to go on tour with Pramatha: camp life was not new to her as she had gone on many tours with her father, R.C. Dutt, a member of the ICS. The first part of the Boses' journey was by the East India railways to the railhead of Rajnandgaon and then by bullock cart to Raipur. Kamala wrote in her memoir that the only way to access the 'deep forest' where the tents were to be pitched was on horseback. For the young woman who had never climbed on to a horse, riding side-saddle was the only option. Entire households moved during camp – the entourage being carted on 'the baggage train' of several pack animals. In this instance, the government provided camels to transport luggage and household items as well as the retinue of servants. Furniture and personal effects, 'thunder boxes' (portable commodes), iron bathtubs and buckets as well as a substantial stock of food supplies were essential and Kamala added that tinned edibles were indispensable. Camps were pitched at intervals of 10–15 miles, and each stop was only of a few days. Six months in the year were spent on tour and the rest in Calcutta.

During the first year, the couple traversed the region by the banks of the river Narmada; after dark, Pramatha would adopt the role of amateur ethnographer and discuss with the local Koli and Bhil tribals their customs and way of life. Kamala was witness to these discussions, all of which she enjoyed. On the next trip, her infant son of three months, Ashok, was put in a makeshift bassinet and carried on the back of porters; his milk was stored in bottles and he would be put down at periodic intervals and fed under the shade of a tree. With sundown, came fears associated with the jungle: 'at night, often, from within the tent, we would hear the call of a tiger … I used to fear that the tiger would tear through the flimsy canvas of the tent and carry my infant off'. Kamala would clutch Ashok close to her as the roars reverberated through the forest on such long nights.

At a distance from the camp was a deep waterbody, the group had been provided with an elephant to cross it. With the elephant came a mahout and two helpers to cook chapattis, cut and collect fodder and so on. One day, as the *atta* ran short, there were no chapattis for the behemoth. The enraged animal shook his body so vigorously that the helper fell into a particularly deep part of the murky water. An agitated mahout tried to rescue the hapless man who by now was entangled in weeds and slime. The only option was to take the elephant to the rescue – but, come what may, he refused to budge. Nor were the available ropes long enough to reach the drowning man. Kamala wrote, 'In this manner, the unfortunate man drowned in front of our eyes and we watched helplessly. That evening, when

An open cookhouse at a campsite. Photograph, c. 1930s

chapattis were prepared for the elephant and he was to be fed in front of my husband and myself, he refused to eat them. Large tears rolled out of his eyes. We were amazed at the sight!' And when it was time to go and look for the body of the helper in the water, this time the repentant elephant was more than willing.

Though Kamala did not have any more such painful experiences during her touring years, she certainly had to face the challenge of taking small children with her. Yet, as she reported, 'It is indeed surprising that though over all these years, six months were spent wandering in the deep jungles', nobody got really ill. On one occasion, however, when her son, Alok, had convulsions and had to be 'rushed' to the nearest hospital 30 miles away, Kamala sat with him in a makeshift *doolie* carried by coolies while Ashok and Pramatha rode alongside. Would Pramatha have written about an elephant's remorse, the tantrums of a maverick camp attendant or having to deal with the situation when the last available ounce of the baby's milk has curdled? Or would his accounts contain copious details of geological strata and different terrains, a faithful account of what he had set out to do? The answer is the latter probably, and it was left to Kamala's ingenuousness to bring such journeys and adventures alive. Nor was she alone in this as is clear from many women's memoirs that deal with what is today known as coping and damage control.

Cover of India Revisited *by Edwn Arnold, 1886*

A THIRSTY
ADVENTURER

⚡

*P*art of the colonial enterprise involved keeping those back home informed of – if not titillated by – the Raj at work. Accounts of various aspects of British rule in India became popular, some racy and exciting, narrated by skilled raconteurs, others more prosaic and factual: the social life of the colonisers, stories, real as well as fictional, of their adjustment to an extreme climate, alien culture, servants and encounters with so-called 'native' cunning and servility as well as memoirs by district officials, judges, lawyers and housewives were eagerly awaited. Poring over family photo albums, scrapbooks and journals fuelled many evenings of nostalgia and vicarious interest. Newspaper articles on India that dealt not only with 'hard' news but also experiences of various kinds evidently had a committed readership. Though all authors may not have had the Kiplingesque touch, many had a story or two to tell.

Edwin Arnold, known best for *The Light of Asia*, his poetic rendering of the life and teachings of the Buddha, also wrote for the popular media. In 1856, he became principal of Sanskrit (later Deccan) College at Poona (Pune) and a Fellow of Bombay University. When he left India in 1862, the academic-cum-journalist was proficient in Sanskrit, Persian, Arabic, and Turkish. In London, Arnold soon joined *The Daily Telegraph* of which he was

The Mutha River, south of Poona. Photograph, c. 1930s

to become editor. Years later, he wrote an article in the paper about 'A Real Thirst', when, in 1860, he had ridden up from his home in Poona to the hill station of Mahabuleshwar (Mahabaleshwar), a distance 'considerably over 100 miles by the Sattara [Satara] route'. Arnold distinguished the thirst he experienced from 'the very ordinary feeling that arises after hearty exercise'. What he had felt under the hot Indian sky was very different: 'the want of something to moisten the parched throat and fill the dried and burning veins transcends all limit of wish or desire, and becomes an agony probably far keener than any arising from hunger'.

As the railways had just about come to the country, the usual mode of travel to any distance for the likes of Arnold was by carriage or on horseback, both known as 'laying a dak'. The carriage, of course, was 'a rattle-trap vehicle' called a *shigram* – the irony unmistakable in the use of a word that meant 'swift'. A long journey on horseback involved meticulous planning ahead of time. A Parsi contractor in the bazaar who also dealt in horses would place animals along the way at a distance of 12 miles or 'six *koss*'. Not particularly well bred and 'full of every kind of vice' (Arnold delicately avoids elucidating on these), they nevertheless did the job at an easy canter.

Choosing to do the first part of the journey on his own little Arab, Arnold was happy to take to his familiar saddle after 'hard work at the College'. He observed the butterflies, a group of 'seven brown sisters … green paroquets [*sic*]', kites and vultures circling a-high. And then the cobra at home under a huge stone, near a temple, basking in the sun as he rode quietly by. Nobody would harm 'the old grey snake, which I had often seen before, and passed by that afternoon as usual, not interfering with his harmless solitude'. The second shift was on a Deccan pony, and his role over, Mr Brown was led home by Arnold's syce. Every change of pony was not stress-free as often the mounts resisted being saddled, kicking and biting in the process.

Despite the little-inhabited terrain, Edwin Arnold thought nothing of riding through the night as jackals stole 'like shadows across the fields'. However, he had to slow down his pace as the route became steeper and more tortuous. Exhausted, he fell asleep on a grassy knoll, only to be awakened by a brilliant Indian dawn when the *Dam-i-subh* or the 'breath of morning' swept by 'like the sigh of the great earth turning and waking'. For some reason, Arnold had ventured forth on his journey with only a bottle of soda water, and when he saw the gleam of the river Krishna far below, he felt sure he would get basics such as milk, eggs and, of course, water to slake his growing thirst. However, the area was in the grip of a cholera epidemic and rather than attend to his needs, desperate survivors asked him whether he was 'a hakim, a vaidya, a doctor'. As he was none of these and had no medicines to offer, he rode on to the nearest *dak* bungalow. As he dismounted, his restless pony drove him against a post, shattering his precious bottle of soda water. There was no *chowkidar* in sight – he too had been a victim of the epidemic; though the river looked tempting, Arnold desisted as he knew that 'every ripple … must have been full of cholera-germ'. With little option, he lay down on a charpoy till it was cool enough to ride on.

After almost a day had passed without a drink of water, Arnold experienced what he called 'the second phase of thirst' when it was 'a passion and a pain' to be without water. There was little option but to go on and as he did not quite know the way, he asked a peasant how he could get to Mahabuleshwar. A costly mistake, as the town was known as Malcom

Peth locally – and his guide sent him off to a temple, thinking that that was what Arnold was looking for: he was not wrong in doing so as a literal translation of Mahabuleshwar is 'the place of the great Lord of Strength'.

Two and a half hours later the worthy professor was well and truly lost in a jungle where he 'heard much too plainly for my comfort upon the left the sharp quick cough that tiger gives when he is calling to his mate'. He wearily entered a hut – only to recoil from a dead body on the charpoy. Back in the jungle, it was not possible to hunt even for fruit in the moonless night; his head ached, he was feverish, and with a throat 'like blistered parchment', Arnold's desperation mounted.

Finally, he was fortunate enough to be discovered by a couple of woodcutters on their way home; Arnold was barely able to explain his situation to them – but they understood enough to guide him to a bungalow where two men sat with a lamp and a table with glasses and beer bottles. Unable to greet his 'hosts', the exhausted man pointed to his throat and the unopened bottle. As one of them poured the foaming liquid down his throat 'every drop seemed a veritable elixir of life'. No names or greetings were exchanged between the men who only shook hands when they parted company; as Edwin Arnold headed off in the direction of his anxious friends, he concluded that to be as thirsty as he had been was quite enough for an entire lifetime. Yet, a vivid recounting of his thirst-filled anguish would have provided the smog-bound London reader a real-life adventure of sorts to dwell on. Bright sunshine, misted hilltops, a cobra, cholera-ridden bodies and perhaps a tiger lurking somewhere in that eerie night in an Indian jungle – could one ask for much more? And as all this was on horseback, Arnold's article was bound to be an instant success among a people committed to equestrian pursuits – even if the steed in question was no more than a mangy hill pony.

VOYAGES OUT

*I*n large parts of India, a variety of waterborne vessels traversed the
many water courses, where dangers of another kind were to be
confronted. Shipwrecks and the occasional pirate are mentioned
many a time in autobiographies and in fiction. Interestingly, riverine modes
of transportation gave some women a certain freedom. Kailashbashini
Debi's *Janaika Grihabadhur Diary* (A Certain Housewife's Diary) describes
long journeys by boat with her husband, Kishory Chand Mitter where
'we used to play cards'. He was in the service of the East India Company
and had made it a point to educate his eleven-year-old bride at home,
even employing an Englishwoman for the purpose. On his tours, Kishory
Chand chose to take his *purdahnashin* wife with him – the relative privacy of
the boat gave the couple the opportunity to grow close, a privilege hardly
possible in the carefully monitored environs of the joint family home.

Though comfortable in her riverine abode, Kailashbashini does not
describe the vessel and it is left to Bishop Heber to write about what he
calls the 'Bengalee boat'. The cabin that occupied almost two-thirds of the
deck was a light bamboo and straw structure, 'exactly like a small cottage
without a chimney'. The passengers sat and slept here and as its roof was
too fragile, another, sturdier, platform above it was built for the boatmen.
Long bamboos with circular boards at the end served as oars and another
one as the mast pole. 'Nothing,' commented Heber 'can seem more clumsy

'Tolly's Nulla, near Kidderpore (Calcutta)'
Carte de visite *photograph by Westfield & Co., c. 1860s*

and dangerous than these boats … but with a fair wind they will sail over the water merrily'.

In later 19th- and early 20th-century India, for the handful who crossed the *kala pani*, the black waters that led to the unknown, and wrote about their experiences, a description of the sea voyage was an accepted entrée. Few however, wrote of the excitement of boarding a ship incognito. In March 1868, when he was only nineteen, R.C. Dutt ran away from home under cover of darkness to board a steamer bound for England. Surendranath Banerjea, who left with the permission of his family, booked berths for 'two friends': Dutt and B.L. Gupta. All three were going to London to compete for the ICS examination, just opened to Indians. Despite heavy odds, the three young men became the second lot of Indians to join the 'heaven born service': the fact that they had crossed the seas in what 'our wisest friends would have considered … madness to venture in an impossible undertaking' brought in long-term dividends at a time when social ostracism on their return was inevitable.

MEMORIES OF BELONGING

By the beginning of the 20th century, the *kala pani* was deemed to have shed some of its evil influence. In 1906, Oriya educationist, Sailabala Das, travelled to England on board the P&O's *Moldavia* and narrated at length her fifteen-day journey in *Bilat Prabas* (Sojourn in England). Sailabala, then thirty-two, was on her way to Maria Grey Training College in London for an advanced teacher's training degree and her meticulous documentation of life aboard the steamer would suggest that she was an assiduous diarist and perhaps a committed letter writer.

On her sea voyage organised by Thomas Cook, Sailabala had two companions, Saralabala Mitra and Fatima Fyzee, who were also on their way to study. The liner was on six levels, and Sailabala and Sarala were allotted well-appointed rooms on the fifth level reserved for first-class passengers. Sailabala writes, 'On every bed lay a soft feather-filled mattress covered with clean milk-white bed sheets … an almirah, cabinet and wash basin'. The two women shared the same cabin and used the other as a dressing room. Fearing the heat when they reached the Red Sea, the enterprising Sailabala soon had their cabin fitted with an electric fan. A tour of the ship 'filled us with boundless admiration for the brilliance and ingenuity of the British. On board there were a laundry, a shop selling bread, a dispensary, and a post office' as the vessel was a mail carrier. The ship's parlour had musical instruments, a writing desk, paper, ink, chairs and cushioned couches. For those who wanted to read, there were two glass almirahs full of books.

However, there were culinary issues for the few Indians aboard: when Sarala and Sailabala sat down to eat in the oak-panelled dining hall, they found that 'many types of animals and birds had been killed and cooked with English spices in order to prepare a proper English meal'. Not unexpectedly, the cuisine was not to their taste and the two felt 'discontented'. They were delighted when they spotted two 'black' men among the passengers – though they thought it inappropriate to befriend them. An Indian maid assigned to them was obviously a willing and voluble informant, filling the Indians in with interesting details about the other non-Indian women on board. They were appalled that the English passengers ate lying in bed, 'not bothering to have a wash. We are never used to eat anything before brushing our teeth'. The arrangements for bathing met with Sailabala's exacting Indian standards: in each of the separate bathrooms for men and for women 'there were three tubs, one containing hot sea water, another, cool sea water, and third, cool fresh water. One could take a bath in whichever tub one liked. The time for baths was from early morning to nine a.m.'

As the days wore on, more and more room-weary people appeared on the deck, Sailabala established that there were forty first-class passengers on the ship which 'included a few Sahibs, who were highly placed officials in the judicial department. They were accompanied by three white ladies'. Freed from the regimentation of racial segregation, the three women soon befriended the memsahibs and one day, one of them said to Sailabala, 'I am curious to find out if women of your country want to talk to us or socialize with us. I get the feeling that they dislike us'. An unfazed Sailabala replied, 'You are absolutely mistaken. Of course, they want to socialize with you, but they hold back for fear that you may look down on them. These days people of your country despise our race so much and treat us so shabbily that we get the impression that they never want to be friends with us. This is why we maintain distance from you'. Not to be outdone, the memsahib said, 'Men in your country do not treat their wives well. They shut them up in their houses, and do not let them meet with anyone else! For this reason, men in our country do not respect Indian men and misbehave with them'. Sailabala retorted tartly, 'On this matter our views will never coincide. So we should not carry the argument any further.' The topic was changed and '[we] discussed other things'. Thus ended a brief interracial contretemps.

Sailabala observed that second-class passengers were served food four times a day, whereas first-class passengers ate seven times! They rarely spoke to each other unlike the 'ordinary people' of the second class who, as 'they were not handicapped by the rules of etiquette, they made an effort to know each other'. Though difficulties with the food were not mentioned again, Sailabala was amazed at the voracious appetite of the British, who did full justice to the ample supplies of the ship. On a more sombre note, Sailabala added that if anyone died during the voyage, 'there were arrangements for giving the deceased a Christian burial'. The ship's carpenter would make a coffin that would be weighted down with a heavy iron ball to ensure that it sank to the bottom of the sea. Fortunately, no such eventuality arose –

The first-class dining hall of P&O's SS Moldavia. *Photograph, 1902*

though when Sailabala fell rather ill, her agitated friends called the ship doctor for a visit. He assured them 'that there was no question of my being given a burial at sea'.

After docking at Marseilles on September 14, it was time to say goodbye and entrain for Calais and a new life. Life on the steamer had helped Sailabala, Sarala and Fatima understand a bit of the culture they were soon to encounter. A not inconsequential advantage for a woman like Sailabala who took little time to observe that 'the English in India and the English at home are two different races'.

The Lucknow Express leaving the Cawnpore (Kanpur) station
Photograph, 1915

'FLYING ENGINE
WITH ITS
MIGHTY RATTLE'

⁓

*R*eginald Heber died in 1826, almost three decades before the railways came to India. As quite a bit of his writing deals with the process of getting from place to place, one wonders how he would have written his travelogue while adjusting to the certain predictability of trains as against the constant surprises of the road and the river. Or maybe Heber would have eschewed the engine and continued with traditional modes of transportation that helped the missionary be in touch with a far wider range of people and places. Fanny Parkes too traversed north India by boat, pony cart and palanquin; had she visited a couple of decades later, she would surely have been one of the first women to board a railway carriage.

Deliberations around the introduction of railways in India had lasted ten years, covering several pages of correspondence and documentation, often tiresome in their prolixity. Finally, on April 16, 1853 at 3:35 pm, as three locomotives named variously Sindh, Sultan and Sahib hauled fourteen passenger coaches out of a modest structure at Bori Bunder (today's Chhatrapati Shivaji Terminus or CST) in Bombay, the city was linked to Thana (Thane), 21 miles or 34 kilometres away. This was the first section of the Great Indian Peninsula

The first train on Dapoorie Viaduct. Photograph, 1853

Railway (GIPR). More than a year later, in February 1855, a carriage rolled out of what was then Howrah Station, a motley collection of huts and sheds, to the coalfields of Ranigunge. Madras Presidency inaugurated the Madras Railway the following year and the city was linked to Arcot, 63 miles away. By 1868, the GIPR was on its way to Delhi, and had reached Jubbalpore (Jabalpur); the Bengal-Nagpur Railway (BNR) inched towards Nagpur, and Sholapur, about 150 miles beyond Poona (Pune), was connected, ushering travellers in the direction of Madras and south India.

The railway station was a landmark, that soon identified a village, town or city, the anonymity of the railway platform and the sheds that constituted the station, were clearly spaces of relative freedom. While, in the 1860s, there were some embarrassed noises on how stations needed to be primarily functional, there seemed little reigning in of architects and engineers. From Lucknow to Delhi, even small stations exhibited considerable architectural detail, with Indo-Islamic domes lending atmosphere to what was otherwise 'a sensible functionalism'.

From the point of view of governance, apart from the movement of goods and personnel, the railways made relocation of troops easier – as was evident in 1857–58. Stations were significant punctuation marks in the growing network of tracks – and it was important to ensure that these were safe spaces and railway lines, bridges and tunnels were also secure. Thus, the grim, fortified station at Lahore. Others, though formidable, were nevertheless splendid architectural sights, such as Victoria Terminus in Bombay. In part like an Oxford College, its walls are emblazoned with monkey gargoyles as well as frescoes of steam engines. F.W. Stevens, the engineer who conceived of this grand structure, clearly had a definite view of empire.

As the latter half of the 19th century became a world on the move, an enterprising new generation of Indian travellers boarded trains; in the process, they had to adjust to a faster pace of life and a changed visual economy. Relative speed limited opportunities to observe closely nature and the countryside; as the network of rivers, pathways, dirt tracks, and later tarred roads shared space with the new symbol of imperial progress, passengers had less time and occasion to observe the world that now sped by. Reminiscing about his childhood, the civil servant-cum-historian, R.C. Dutt, wrote about those 'happy pre-railway days when a journey from district to district was performed by palki or boat ... though one travelled less one saw more of the country ... more villages, bazars [sic], and towns, the rivers, ghats and temples'. Many, however, would have been happy to trade in visual pleasures for speed and proximity.

Though in the long run the railways greatly benefited the local population, the initial days were terrifying for many: normally a callous observer of the hapless 'native', the photographer, Samuel Bourne, who traversed north India by train in the 1860s, could not help but have some sympathy for those for whom the train was 'an incarnation of the devil' – petrified villagers ran helter-skelter as they 'beheld the flying engine with its mighty rattle' furrowing 'through their peaceful territory'. In no time, though, not only did the train radicalise travel but also the railway system soon became a way of life, an employer and a rich source for real and fictional adventures and fantasies.

Bridge on Chappar Rift near Mangi, Sind–Pishin Railway
Photograph, 1910

The more enterprising were prepared to try their hand at what was on offer, in the late 1850s, the otherwise feckless Prandhan Banerjee, nephew of the *kulin* widow, Nistarini Debi, enrolled in a nine-month course to learn telegraphic Morse transmission for use in the railways. He was soon employed at Halisahar. In *Sekeley Katha*, her dictated autobiography, Nistarini, who was living with Prandhan at the time, writes of fearful days in the rest room in the makeshift station, surrounded by semi-jungle and the local drunks. Things were a bit better for Jim Corbett, just out of school in the 1890s. He was employed as fuel inspector with the railways on Rs 100 a month. Clearly his job description was a euphemism, as he had to live in the forests of modern-day Bihar, supervising as well as cutting hundreds of cubic feet of timber to be used as fuel by the locomotives.

When, eighteen months later, coal was introduced (and the trees spared), Jim became a general dogsbody, 'at times on the footplates of locomotives', driving engines and even filling in as a guard for goods trains. Stories of a pristine integrity and loyalty are narrated with meticulous Corbettian detail: a railway sweeper who rescues a suitcase full of jewels, Christmas celebrated without any thought for caste or religion and the frontiers of life extended amidst these looming symbols of a new era.

However, it had not been an easy time for those in charge of bringing railways to India. High levels of morbidity and mortality affected workforces, with malaria and cholera being almost endemic. The timely delivery of supplies depended on shipments from Britain – and here too, at least one per cent of vessels were lost at sea. Bridge designs and the wood for sleepers (oblong pieces of wood used as a base for railroad tracks) varied from region to region. The first railway bridge was built over Thane Creek in 1854 and the construction of bridges, tunnels, railway crossings and stations required skill, innovation and a formidable stretch to what was possible.

Bridge engineers had to work out how to build structures on surfaces that may actually be silt for almost a 100 feet; then there was the question of keeping the river under the bridge even when it changed course, to say nothing of the surging monsoons that threatened many a bank. Despite all these travails, hardy railway bridges have invariably survived and many of them are still in use such as the bridge across the Chappar Rift in Balochistan (Pakistan). This region with its extremely challenging terrain was put on the railway map in 1883. Though fewer in number, tunnels involved far greater ingenuity and, often, the supervision of experienced British tunnellers. Normally constructed in hazardous sites, specially trained workers were required, and though blasting and excavation were not unknown to Indian workers, safety conditions were not optimal.

The class and caste system carried on in the railways with first-class travel reserved primarily for Europeans and some select Indians and though there was some effort to make third-class travel more acceptable, in 1866, a petition with 3,000 signatures from the influential British India Association – a lobby group of Indian landowners – berated the government for imposing 'a dire evil and slavery' on that category of travellers. Waiting rooms were non-existent, restaurant cars only for first-class passengers and lavatories hopelessly inadequate and defective in structure. Mohandas Karamchand Gandhi had a piquant relationship with the railways – though his commitment to the cause of Indians in South Africa dated back to his being thrown out of a first-class compartment in Pietermaritzburg on the objection a white passenger, in India he became an indefatigable third-class passenger. He also wrote extensively to the railway authorities on abject conditions in that class: overcrowding, lack of hygiene, ticketless travelling. It was not until 1905 that lavatories were provided for all railway travellers of all classes – though as late as the 1930s photographer T.S. Satyan writes in his memoirs, what the British 'euphemistically' called third class, was infested with bugs of all kinds.

By 1900, nearly 25,000 miles of railway lines had been laid in India and without doubt the system had an important role to play in connecting parts of the country – and hence building the nation. Gradually, the railways became a way of life not only for those who travelled but also for its employees. Well-planned railway colonies were built with special facilities, schools, hospitals and shopping complexes, and many will recall balmy evenings on the deep verandas of the B.N.R. Hotel at Puri, begun in 1924 when the thirty-four-roomed Ashworth House Estate was bought from a Dr Elmes by the Bengal Nagpur Railway. The depression of the thirties, then the outbreak of Second World War – when India became the base for the offensive against Japan and a large number of railway workshops had to be diverted to the manufacture of ammunitions – and finally the partition of the country in 1947, affected the expansion and development of the railway system. That was, of course, a long time ago, and today the Indian railway network system is among one of the largest in the world, connecting the dots on this large and varied canvas of people and places.

WONDER
AND
MELANCHOLY

⌒⟋⟍

A railway journey was not an enviable experience for all: the
train became another site for racial segregation and while the
Europeans travelled in first-class compartments, most Indians
were crammed into the third class, with little access to water and sanitary
facilities. In fact, it would not be too fanciful to imagine an early train as
India in microcosm: the rulers cocooned in luxury, a few privileged Indians
their neighbours in a compartment (though perhaps not in real life), and
the majority of passengers in second and, more likely, third-class carriages.
And life aboard a train for Europeans and a handful of privileged Indians
could indeed be luxurious. Lady Rosamond Lawrence, wife of civilian
Henry Lawrence, writes of train journeys in the early 20th century where
their official saloon 'was shifted from train to train as desired'. There was a
bedroom, a bathroom, and a kitchen, in addition to the public area furnished
with chairs and couches. A few coaches down was another story where the
general carriages, wrote Kipling in 'A Railway Settlement', 'are just now
horrid – being filthy and unshaven, dirty to look at and dirty to live in'.

Over a 150 years later, cynics might ask, has anything really changed for the vast majority of Indian rail travellers?

Among the many stories early passengers had to tell, a favourite theme was surely about encounters with those one was unlikely to run into otherwise. In her autobiography, the Oriya educationist Sailabala Das narrates with some relish her face off with English passengers on a journey from Calcutta to Cuttack. Sensing that she may have problems getting a berth in a first-class compartment, Sailabala sent her *khansama* ahead with the bedding, instructing him to spread it out on a lower berth in the ladies' compartment. Soon enough the *chaprasis* of the travelling English family arrived and, disconcerted to see Sailabala's luggage, reported the situation to their master. Sailabala writes, 'the gentleman got quite red in the face, sent for the guard and asked him to turn the native woman (me) out and tell her to travel in the third class'. The embarrassed guard could say little when he looked at Sailabala's first-class ticket. Not one to let matters rest, Sailabala 'did not mind being called a "native woman" for I am a native woman and proud of it'. But she was insulted by the Englishman's tone and 'wanted to punish them'. She quickly changed her *khansama*'s and ayah's tickets into first-class ones and watched with glee the consternation on the faces of her fellow passengers who then tried their luck with the station master – but to no avail.

Confusion prevailed and as the memsahib shouted out, 'Alec, Alec my dear, see the feet of the native servant dangling just above your head', a distraught Alec tried to barge into the more conducive ladies' compartment. Imagine Sailabala's triumph when she instructed the guard to turn the man out of the ladies' compartment – 'I strongly objected to his travelling in the same compartment as me', she reported smugly. The final denouement, however, was an apology when the Englishman, who turned out to be the district magistrate of Cuttack, discovered that she was the daughter of the well-respected M.S. Das. And as a mollified Sailabala reports this too with some pride, we are reminded that the incident did take place a 100 years ago when demonstration of regret from an Englishman was no mean thing.

As the railways opened up new, uninhabited areas, it was important to provide for the security of trains, railway lines, bridges, and tunnels. Railway

Khojak Tunnel

'Khojak Tunnel'
Photograph by Fred Bremner, 1905

lines often traversed difficult terrains, through dense jungles and across mutinous rivers. In Kipling's 'The Bridge Builders', Findlayson turns to opium at the thought of his months of perilous labour and supervision being destroyed by an early flood. Being photographed while at work (and building the railway system was no small task) had gained in popularity by the closing years of the 19th century. It was important to remind the family and posterity of what constructing the empire had meant, and men were quick to underline the hazardously unknown aspects of such work.

Nor were these emotions entirely absent among train passengers. An ambience of slight uncertainty, a latent tension combined with some underlying excitement was common. And often there were serendipitous encounters, not always of the most welcome kind: theft and pilferage became rampant in the railways and often after a robbery, hapless victims were reluctant to report it. Not only had fear of the police network and its unkind ways of functioning become a part of the mythology surrounding the colonial State, but also victims had no common language in which to express themselves. Imagine a Bihari worker on his way to try his luck in Bombay Presidency being robbed in the forbidding thuggee-infested badlands of Central India; while broken Hindustani may have got him some mileage with the local police, it would hardly be enough for him to be able to say where, when and how he had been robbed, if not mugged. Would he have known the route and stations that the train had passed through in the dead of night? Unlikely. Not unexpectedly then, a 1904 Joint Commission on Interprovincial Crime in Assam, Bengal and the United Provinces identified the railways as the most significant reason for the alarming rise in theft in this region. Used to a stationary population, the police force was hard put to ferret out 'mobile' thieves.

As one would expect, children, particularly those who travelled in the first class, were immune to such grown-up fears; for them, there was little to rival a train ride. Colonial memoirs recount many such journeys, some more exciting than others. A few write of the discomfort, others marvel at platforms – teeming with an endless stream of people jostling for space with monkeys, dogs and even donkeys. It is doubtful whether the engineers who constructed the grand stations of British India had ever envisioned the many uses the wide platforms would be put to. Dormitory, recreation centre, worship space, food mall, playground, bookshop – who can ever deny the varied life of the Indian railway platform.

Jon and Rumer Godden write of long train journeys to north Indian hill stations. As high-spirited children, they swung from the upper berths, visited the lavatory endlessly – assiduously disinfected with Lysol by their mother – and waited for entertainment at the next station. Ample food lay safe in tiffin baskets, 'large oblong Japanese cane baskets with leather strappings to hold enamel plates and mugs'. Bottled water was carried from home and though during the journey, 'bread went dry, butter melted, shells off the hard-boiled eggs got into the buttoned upholstery of the bunk seats … we thought the meal ambrosial'. An accompanying servant would come to wash up, squatting on the floor of the lavatory shower room that led off from the compartment. In the blazing hot summer when travelling in what were basically metal boxes on wheels could be unbearable, a zinc stand with a deep tray beneath it was set up in the middle of the compartment 'and

'Bombay-Poona Mail, Great Indian Peninsula Rly'
Postcard by Raphael Tuck & Sons, 1920

every morning with shoutings and staggerings, coolies would carry in a huge block of ice and unwrap it from its sacking'. A fan often circulated the cooled air and telegrams used to be sent down the line for replacements of ice during the day.

As dusk came about the countryside, 'a curious sadness would fall on us' and the compartment suddenly seemed small, 'the train infinitesimal as it travelled over the vast Indian plain'. And then finally, out came the bedding from those 'invaluable roly-poly pieces of luggage rightly called holdalls into which anything and everything would go'. Those irreplaceable holdalls may be difficult to come by today, and ice blocks have given way to fitful air conditioning; yet which train passenger can deny an inexplicable sense of wonderment – or maybe even melancholy – as night falls, a few lights twinkle on the horizon and the edges of India fade away beneath the criss-cross of railway tracks?

Glossary

adda	verbal conversations and discussions among a group of friends or equals
athchala	eight-roofed temple
atta	wheat flour
attar	a fragrant essential oil made usually from rose petals
ayah	children's maid
babalog	Western and/or Anglicised children and young people
bagh	garden
bajra	millet
bandobast	arrangements
barasingha	Kashmir stag
bhisti	water carrier
bhujia	fried vegetables
budgerow	country boat
chapatti	unleavened bread made from wheat flour
chaprasi	peon
charpoy	rustic cot with rope webbing
chawls	lower-income tenements
chowkidar	watchman
cutcherry	government offices and law courts
coolie	unskilled manual labourer

coolie *sardar*	contractor hiring out coolies
dak	mail
dandi	a hammock or seat slung on two bamboo poles and carried by two or more men
darshan	the opportunity to see or the occasion of seeing a holy person or the image of a deity
darzi	tailor
dhurna or *dharna*	sit-in
doodwala	milkman
doolie	covered litter
dubash	literally, one who speaks more than one language; interpreter
durbar	court
duree	cotton carpet
gara	Parsi sari
ghat	river bank, hilly area
'gollas'	*gwalas*, cattle-herders
harkara	informant; also runners with *dak*
hakim	traditional doctor of the Unani school
howdah	seat atop an elephant
jamadar	sweeper
jhampan	palanquin-like sedan chair carried by two or more men
jharokha	ornamental overhanging balconies
kala pani	literally, black waters; implies the prejudice associated with crossing the seas – and thereby losing caste
kampung	a small village or community of houses in Malay-speaking areas
kasthalika matha	a Catholic monastery
keora sharbat	sherbet made from distillation of pandanus flowers
khalasi	a manual worker, especially a docker, porter, or sailor
khansama	cook
khitmadgar	table servant
koss, (one)	two miles

kulin	top echelons among the Brahmins of Bengal
kumor	potter
makke ki atta	corn flour
mahout	elephant 'driver' or keeper
mali	gardener
mashal	torch lit by a flame
masula boat	non-rigid boat without any bracing or knees
matan ishtoo	mutton stew
moffusil	non-urban areas
muttram	open courtyard
nautch	traditional dance
neem	*Azadirachta indica*
pakdandi	country path
palki	palanquin
parathas	flat unleavened bread fried on a griddle
patua (*chitrakar*)	painter of images on handmade paper scrolls
pat, patachitras	paintings on handmade paper scrolls
pankha, punkah	fan
peepul	*Ficus religiosa*
purdah	veil, observance of veiling
purdahnashin	one who observes purdah
salwar kameez	a long tunic worn over a pair of baggy, trouser-like lower garment, traditionally worn by women in north India, Pakistan and Afghanistan
sarso	mustard
sati	widow immolation
shikar	hunt
shikari	hunter
shikara	type of wooden boats used on waterways in Kashmir
shigram	fast-paced
sudreh	Parsi undershirt
syce	horse-boy

terai	forest and grassland in the lower foothills
thalvaram	a public veranda along the street
thinnai	a semi-private veranda
tonga	light two-wheeled vehicle drawn by horses or oxen
tonjon	an open sedan chair on a single pole carried on men's shoulders
vaidya	traditional doctor of the Ayurvedic school
zamindar	landlord
zenana	inner women's quarters in a house

Select Bibliography

Alkazi Collection of Photography, The, *et al. The Artful Pose — Early Studio Photography in Mumbai, c. 1855-1940*. Ahmedabad: Mapin Publishing Pvt. Ltd, 2010.

_____. *Mastering the Lens — Before and After Cartier-Bresson in Pondicherry*. Ahmedabad: Mapin Publishing Pvt. Ltd, 2012.

Allana, Rahaab. 'Performance for Camera — Shapoor N. Bhedwar and the Dimensions of Studio Photography in Bombay' in *The Artful Pose — Early Studio Photography in Mumbai, c. 1855-1940*. Ahmedabad: Mapin Publishing Pvt. Ltd, 2010.

Arnold, Edwin. *India Revisited*. London: Kegan Paul, Trench, Trubner and Co. Ltd, 1891.

_____. *East and West: Being Papers Reprinted from the Daily Telegraph and Other Sources*. US: Kessinger Publishing, 2005.

Axelby, Richard. 'Calcutta Botanic Garden and the colonial re-ordering of the Indian environment'. *Archives of natural history* 35(1) (2008): 150–163.

Bayly, C. A. *Empire and Information — Intelligence Gathering and Social Communication in India, 1780-1870*. Cambridge: Cambridge University Press, 1996.

Bentley, Richard. *Life in Bombay and the Neighbouring Out-stations*. London: Richard Bentley, 1852.

Bhandari, Rajika. *The Raj on the move – Story of the Dak Bungalow*. New Delhi: Lotus Collection/Roli Books, 2012.

Bose, Kamala. *Sadhvi Kamala Boser Atmajibani*. n.d.

Bourne, Samuel. Writings in *British Journal of Photography* (1863-1870).

————. 'Ten Weeks with the Camera in the Himalayas'. In *British Journal of Photography* (1864): 50–51.

Corbett, Jim. 'Life at Mokameh Ghat'. In *My India*. New Delhi: Oxford University Press, 2006 [1952].

Das, Sailabala. From *A Look Before and After* (Autobiography) and from *Bilat Prabas* (Sojourn in England). In *Early Women's Writings in Orissa, 1898-1950*, edited by Sachidananada Mohanty. New Delhi: SAGE Publications, 2005.

Debi, Kailashbashini. *Janaika Grihabadhur Diary*. In *Atmakatha*, Vol. II, edited by N.C. Jana, M. Jana and K.K. Sanyal. Calcutta: Ananya Publications, 1982.

Debi, Nistarini. *Sekeley Katha*. In *Atmakatha*, Vol. II, edited by N.C. Jana, M. Jana and K.K. Sanyal. Calcutta: Ananya Publications, 1982.

de Courcy, Anne. *The Fishing Fleet: Husband-Hunting in the Raj*. London: Weidenfeld & Nicolson, 2012.

Dash, Mike. *Thug: The True Story of India's Murderous Cult*. London: Granta, 2005.

Desmond, Ray. *The European Discovery of Indian Flora*. Oxford: Oxford University Press, 1992.

Dhar, Sheila. *'Here's Someone I'd Like You to Meet'*. New Delhi: Oxford University Press, 1995.

Douglas-Home, Jessica. *A Glimpse of Empire*. New Delhi: Rain Tree, 2012.

Dutt, R.C. *Rambles in India: During Twenty-four Years, 1871 to 1895*. Calcutta: S.K. Lahiri, 1895.

Gokhale, Namita. *Mountain Echoes – Reminiscences of Kumaoni Women*. New Delhi: Roli Books, 1998.

Godden, Jon and Rumer. *Two Under the Indian Sun*. London: Macmillan and company, 1966.

Gupta, J.N. *Life and Work of R.C. Dutt*. London: J.M. Dent and Sons, 1911.

Heber, Reginald. *Narrative of a Journey through the Upper Provinces of India from Calcutta to Bombay, 1824–1825*, Vols I & II. London: John Murray, 1873.

Herbert, Eugenia W. *Flora's Empire – British Gardens in India*. New Delhi: Allen Lane, 2013.

Howes, Jennifer. *Illustrating India – The Early Colonial Investigations of Colin Mackenzie (1784-1821)*. New Delhi: Oxford University Press, 2010.

Jaffrey, Madhur. *Climbing the Mango Trees – A Memoir of a Childhood in India*. London: Random House, 2006.

Jayewardene-Pillai, Shanti. *Imperial Conversations: Indo-Britons and the Architecture of South India*. New Delhi: Yoda Press, 2007.

Karlekar, Malavika. *Visual Histories: Photography in the Popular Imagination*. New Delhi: Oxford University Press, 2013.

Kennedy, Dane. *The Magic Mountains: Hill Stations and the British Raj*. New Delhi: Oxford University Press, 1996.

Khan, Omar. *From Kashmir to Kabul – The Photographs of John Burke and William Baker, 1860–1900*. Ahmedabad: Mapin Publishing Pvt. Ltd, 2002.

Khanduri, Ritu. 'Vernacular Punches: Cartoons and Politics in Colonial India'. *History and Anthropology* 20(4) (December 2009): 459–486.

King, Anthony. *The Bungalow – The Production of a Global Culture*. London: Routledge and Kegan Paul, 1984.

Kipling, Rudyard. *The Phantom Rickshaw and other stories*. New York: Charles Scribner's Sons, 1899.

_____. *Among the Railway Folk*. http://ebooks.adelaide.edu.au/k/kipling/rudyard/railway/complete.html.

Kosambi, Meera. 'British Bombay and Marathi Mumbai: Some Nineteenth

Century Perceptions'. In *Bombay – Mosaic of Modern Culture*, edited by Sujata Patel and Alice Thorner, pp. 3-24. Bombay: Oxford University Press, 1995.

Lambert-Hurley, Siobhan and Sunil Sharma. *Atiya's Journeys – A Muslim Woman from Colonial Bombay to Edwardian Britain*. New Delhi: Oxford University Press, 2010.

Lawrence, Rosamund. *Indian Embers*. Oxford: George Ronald, 1949.

Luther, Narendra. *Raja Deen Dayal – Prince of Photographers*. Hyderabad: HRH, 2003.

Macfarlane, Robert. *Mountains of the Mind – A History of a Fascination*. London: Granta Books, 2003.

Maxwell, Lady Lyle. In *Respected Memsahibs – An Anthology*, compiled by Mary Thatcher. Kilkerran: Hardinge Simpole, 2009.

Menon, K.P.S. *Journey Round the World*. Bombay: Bharatiya Vidya Bhavan, 1966.

Mitter, Partha. 'Cartoons of the Raj'. *History Today* 47(9) (September 1997).

Morris, Jan with Simon Winchester. *Stones of Empire – The Buildings of the Raj*. Oxford: Oxford University Press, 1983.

Mukherjee, Rudrangshu. 'Old seat for a new empire: Calcutta to Delhi'. In *New Delhi: Making of a Capital*, by Malvika Singh and Rudrangshu Mukherjee. New Delhi: Roli Books, 2009.

Oliver, A.K. *The Hill Station of Matheran*. Bombay: Times of India Press, 1905.

Pinney, Christopher. 'Stirred by Photography'. In *Allegory & Illusion – Early Portrait Photography from South Asia*. Ahmedabad: Mapin Publishing Pvt. Ltd and the Alkazi Collection of Photography in association with the Rubin Museum of Art, New York, 2013.

Pols, Robert. *Family Photographs 1860-1945*. London: Public Records Office Publications, 2002.

Preston, Rebecca. "Against This Terrible Invasion of Foreigners We Would Protest". *Cabinet*, Issue 6 Horticulture (2002). http://cabinetmagazine.org/issues/6/index.php.

Ray, Satyajit. 'The Indigo Terror'. Translated from the original '*Neel atanko*' in Bengali by Barnali Saha. http://www.parabaas.com/translation/database/translations/stories/satyajit_indigo.html.

Rycroft, Daniel J. *Representing Rebellion – Visual Aspects of Counter-Insurgency in Colonial India*. New Delhi: Oxford University Press, 2006.

Scidmore, Eliza Ruhamah. *Winter India*. London: T. Fisher Unwin, 1903.

Singer, Andre. *Lords of the Khyber: The Story of the North-West Frontier*. London: Faber and Faber, 1984.

Smith, George. *The Life of William Carey, D.D.: Shoemaker and Missionary*. New York: Cambridge University Press, 2011.

Sontag, Susan. *On Photography*. New York: Delta 1977[1973]

Steel, Flora Annie and Grace Gardiner. *The Complete Indian Housekeeper and Cook*. London: W. Heinemann, 1921 [1888].

Tagore, Debendranath. *Swarachita Jiban Charit* (Autobiography). In *Atmakatha*, Vol. 1, edited by N.C. Jana, *et al*. Calcutta: Ananya Publications, 1981.

Ward, Frank Kingdon. *In the Land of the Blue Poppies*. New York: The Modern Library, 2003.

Younghusband, Sir Francis. *The Heart of Nature or, The Quest for Natural Beauty*. London: John Murray, 1921.

_____. *Kashmir as it was*. New Delhi: Rupa Publications, 2004.

Image Credits

Individuals

Anirban Das Gupta, Kolkata: p. 206

Author's collection: pp. 12, 15, 21, 32, 35, 37, 43, 49, 53, 54, 64, 72, 80, 95, 99, 110, 119, 125, 179, 180, 182, 188, 200

Bikram Grewal, New Delhi: p. 24

Hemant and Minoti Jain, Mumbai: p. 146

Jessica Douglas-Home, UK: p. 86

Late Karam Mayadas, Goa: p. 46

Late Ome Anand, Kaladhungi: pp. 101, 102

Rajat Datta, Kolkata: p. 40

Institutions

Centre of South Asian Studies, University of Cambridge, Cambridge (from the Davey and Maxwell collections): pp. 176, 192

PARZOR, New Delhi: p. 137

Samudri Archives, Chennai: p. 173

The Alkazi Collection of Photography, New Delhi: pp. 147, 149, 156, 159

The J. Paul Getty Museum, Los Angeles: p. 84

Victoria Memorial Hall, Kolkata: pp. 44, 126, 130

Websites

Images of Asia (http://www.imagesofasia.com/):
pp. 16, 92, 104, 116, 117, 141, 142, 144, 162, 166, 168b, 186, 213, 215

Families in British India Society (from Valerie Boddy, estate of Alfred Cecil Gregory) (http://www.wiki.fibis.org/): p. 91

P&O Heritage Website (http://www.poheritage.com/) (P&O Ref: PH-02767-00): p. 203

Wikimedia Commons (http://commons.wikimedia.org/): pp. 26, 78, 174

Wikipedia Commons (http://en.wikipedia.org/): pp. 58a and b, 68

Books

Birds of Asia, Vol. III by John Gould, 1861–66: p. 66

Flora Indica 3 by William Roxburgh, 1932: pp. 61, 120

India Revisited by Edwin Arnold, 1886: pp. 75, 106, 123, 194

Some Beautiful Indian Trees by Ethelbert Blatter and Walter Samuel Millard, 1937: p. 18

The Hill Station of Matheran by Mrs A.K. Oliver, 1905: p. 153

Wonderful India, 1930s: pp. 28, 76, 89, 113, 128, 135, 138, 161, 164, 168a, 171, 190, 196, 204, 208

Acknowledgements

This is the second book that I owe to the generosity of *The Telegraph*, Kolkata and to Rudrangshu Mukherjee. Like *Visual Histories – Photography in the Popular Imagination* the present collection is based on columns for *The Telegraph* – though with one big difference. A larger number have been re-cast and edited far more drastically than in the earlier volume.

I am deeply appreciative of the inputs from readers of the original articles – both known and unknown – who have shared ideas, corrections and images with me. I thank Nitasha Devasar for introducing me to Niyogi Books and Tutltul and Bikash Niyogi for taking on this volume. My editor, Shaurya Shaukat Sircar and I had hardly a quibble for which I am grateful. The design aspect of such a book is always critical, and I owe what I think is an elegant product to Brinda Datta and the production department at Niyogi Books.

My greatest debt is to those individuals and institutions who have shared visuals with me unstintingly. At the top of the list are persons whom I have never met – but thanks to the marvels of the Web, have been able to approach. Omar Khan of www.imagesofasia.com has not only been amazingly generous with sharing a number of postcard images with me but also his prompt response each time was extremely welcome. Hemant and Minoti Jain provided a portrait of their ancestor, the outstanding photographer of the 19th century, Raja Deen Dayal while Anirban Das Gupta found a rare railway image for me. Peter Bailey and Valmay Young of www.fibis.org and Beth Ellis of www.poheritage.com went out of their way to give me rare images at what was close to the eleventh hour. Again, a bit of sleuthing led me to Jessica Douglas-Home who too had no hesitation in sharing an image of her fascinating grandmother, Lilah Wingfield. At the end of the day, I feel that I've made a new circle of friends whom I hope I'll meet someday!

Then of course, there are my old acquaintances: Jawhar Sircar was most helpful in getting permission from Victoria Memorial Hall, Kolkata, while Kevin Greenbank of Centre for South Asian Studies, Cambridge, Rahaab Allana, Shilpi and Jennifer of the Alkazi Collection of Photography and Shernaz Cama of PARZOR responded once more to my requests for permission to use images. Brinda and Bikram did some important sourcing for me and the heirs of Karam Mayadas and Ome Anand too were happy to let me use photos from family albums.

The many images in the book emerged as a result of Sundaresh's patience at the computer and Chinmoy Banerjee's skillful interventions. The search for an appropriate title as well as the rush of last minute editing was made easier for me by Brinda and Hiranmay (Ronu). Brinda went far beyond her mandate as designer to point out clumsy sentences and even edit these, while tweaks at the title by Ronu and Nilanjana S. Roy (Dimpy) were invaluable. I thank them and all those who rallied to my support, often with little time at hand, and hope that they as well my readers, family and friends will enjoy these explorations into our rich visual and textual culture – and share my excitement at being able to spin a tale around words and images.